Canada: Origins and Options

CANADA AND THE WORLD WARS

Canada: Origins and Options

CANADA AND THE WORLD WARS

Author
Iain R. Munro
Faculty of Education
Queen's University

Consulting Authors

Howard A. Doughty
Darrel R. Skidmore

WILEY PUBLISHERS OF CANADA LIMITED
Toronto

To: the memory of my grandfather
Samuel Wilkinson, who knew the
horrors of war; and to my
children, Adrienne Alexandra
Shoshannah Munro and Kyla Anna
Maria Munro — who, like all
children, now deserve a chance
to live in peace and universal
fraternity.

Designers and Illustrators
KB Graphics

Canadian Cataloguing in Publication Data

Munro, Iain R., 1941-
    Canada and the world wars

(Canada, origins and options)

Includes index.
ISBN 0-471-99773-0

1. European War, 1914-1918 — Canada.
2. World War, 1939-1945 — Canada.
3. Canada — History — 1914-1945.
I. Title.   II. Series

FC540.M85   971.06   C79-094185-6
F1034.M85

Printed and Bound in Canada

10 9 8 7 6 5 4 3 2 1

Cover photo: Public Archives of Canada

Foreword to the Series

During the nineteen-seventies students and teachers across Canada have displayed a growing interest in Canadian studies. This book is one in a series that has been designed to encourage the student of social studies to explore our culture and our heritage.

Each book in the series centres on one specific topic. However, all the books share some common objectives.

Their first task is to make Canada comprehensible to students. To accomplish this aim, each book concentrates on only one aspect of our complex society. Thus each book can provide a basic awareness of one set of issues that confront us, and the various options that are open to us.

The second objective is to help students use their basic knowledge to develop into politically aware and knowledgeable citizens. The challenges that confront Canadians today and will confront us in the future are difficult to understand. Only with a firm grasp of our heritage will we as individuals be able to respond creatively to the problems we will encounter in the final quarter of the twentieth century.

Finally, our hope is that this series will contribute to the well-being of our country by helping to create a more informed public. Any society, in order to survive, must be able to adapt to social change. Informed citizens are a necessary condition for any society which hopes to adapt successfully to the changes that are imposed by modern social development.

The conservative historian W. L. Morton once wrote that our experience as Canadians teaches us "that what is important is not to have triumphed but to have endured." Similarly, the poet Margaret Atwood commented that "Canadians are forever taking the national pulse like doctors at a sickbed: the aim is not to see whether the patient will live well but simply whether he will live at all."

If we are to live and to live well, we must begin to know ourselves. These books, we hope, will help to build such self-knowledge.

Howard A. Doughty
Iain R. Munro
Darrel R. Skidmore

Acknowledgements

I would like to express my gratitude for the very thorough evaluations and helpful suggestions provided by G. Hugh Duplisea of Fredericton, New Brunswick; Fred Jarman of Toronto, Ontario; and W.A.B. Douglas of the National Defence Headquarters in Ottawa, Ontario. I am also indebted to James A. W. Rogerson of Wiley Publishers and to our editor, Dee Pennock, for their valuable assistance and enthusiastic support for this project. Finally, I wish to thank my wife and colleague, Heidi Munro, for her generous assistance and discerning advice in the preparation of this book.

Iain R. Munro

CONTENTS

Introduction   8

Are Canadians an
   "Unmilitary" People?   11

Chapter One: **The Nature of War**   12

Why Do Nations Start Wars?   14
Why Do Soldiers Go to War?   16
Summary   27

Chapter Two: **Canada and the First World War**   28

The British Empire Declares
   War   32
Canadians Join the War   34
Canada on the Western Front   36
The Slaughter Continues
   (1915-1916)   39
Vimy Ridge   40
The War in the Air   44
The Bloodbath of Passchendaele   46
The Last 100 Days   46
Armistice Day, November 11,
   1918   47
Summary   49

Chapter Three: **Canada in the Second World War**   50

Origins of the Second World
   War   50
The Rise of Fascism   55

Declarations of War   58
The Canadian War Effort   59
Canada's Air Force and Navy   60
The Dieppe Raid, 1942   62
The Italian Campaign   65
The Normandy Invasion   66
Summary   69

Chapter Four: **Canada on the Home Front**   **70**

Economic Growth   70
How War Affected Canadian
   Women   73
Recruitment   75
Maintaining the War Effort   77
Conscription in World War I   77
Conscription in World War II   81
Ethnic Relations   81
Summary   83

Chapter Five: **Why Do We Remember?**   **84**

The Human Cost of War   88
Civilian Deaths in Wartime   90
Atomic Bombs   90
Summary   93

Glossary   **94**

Index   **95**

Introduction

In the 1960s, the lyrics of a popular folk song said, "I ain't gonna study war no more." Since the beginning of recorded time, human beings have desired and sought after peace. And yet when peace has been achieved, it has seldom lasted for very long. Since 3600 B.C., the world has known only 292 years of peace. During this period, historians have recorded 14 531 wars, both large and small. These wars have killed countless millions of people. As our civilizations have "progressed," people have killed one another with increasing speed and efficiency.

In this century, we have the largest armies of all time, even in proportion to our population. In 1650, an army of 50 000 was large. In the eighteenth century, an army of 100 000 was considered gigantic. By 1814, Napoleon had armies of half a million soldiers. Today, even the peacetime armies of the major world powers number into the millions.

Wars have increased in size and in the number of countries involved. The two great wars of this century have been called "world" wars, because they have involved so many nations of the world.

Modern science has had a tremendous impact on war. Never before have so few been able to kill so many. Atomic bombs which were dropped on two Japanese cities in 1945 — just one bomb on each city — killed 150 000 and injured many more within a few minutes.

It is estimated that the present nuclear stockpile in the United States is sufficient to make 655 000 bombs of this type. Today, one plane in one mission can drop more explosive power than both sides dropped against each other in the five and one-half years of the Second World War.

The possibility of war increases in direct proportion to the effectiveness of the instruments of war.

Norman Cousins

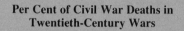

**Per Cent of Civil War Deaths in
Twentieth-Century Wars**

Per Cent of
Civilian Deaths

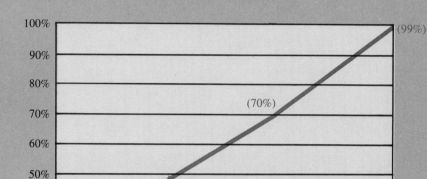

World War I	World War II	Vietnam	Nuclear War

(5%) (48%) (70%) (99%)

The number of civilians killed in any war is at best a rough estimate. This is especially true in Vietnam because of the nature of the warfare. Bombing from the air and artillery fire from many miles away can mean a heavy civilian toll.

By early 1971, the tonnage of bombs dropped in Vietnam was 2½ times that dropped by both sides in all theatres in the Second World War.

It is estimated that 1.5 million persons died in Indochina in 10 years of war, of which the great majority were civilians.

Minimal estimates of deaths from a first-strike nuclear attack are put at 50 million persons, of which only a small per cent would be military personnel.

William A. Nesbitt. *Data on the Human Crisis: A Handbook for Inquiry* (New York: Center for International Programs and Comparative Studies of the New York State Education Department, 1972), p. 13 (Reprinted by permission).

Do people really want peace?

Who suffers from war? Does anyone gain?

Do you think the world can achieve a lasting peace?

Why do wars occur? Why do people fight? Why do nations intentionally inflict destruction and suffering upon other nations? In the first chapter, we will explore some of these questions. We will also examine the nature of war, especially its impact on the individual soldiers. Almost 500 years ago, a Dutch scholar, Desiderius Erasmus, said that "war is delightful to those who have no experience with it." Was he saying it is a horror to those who have participated in it and know its true nature?

It is important to know what war is like and what it can do. Only by understanding this are men and women likely to become committed to finding alternatives to war. If we do not find alternatives, we may not have much time left to us on earth. The great scientist Albert Einstein emphasized this when he said, "The next world war would be fought with stones."

Are Canadians an "Unmilitary" People?

Colonel C.P. Stacey, one of our most important war historians, claims that "Canada is an unmilitary community. Warlike her people have often been forced to be; military they have never been."

While this statement may be disputed in regard to our earlier history, it is true that since Confederation in 1867 Canada is one of the few nations of the world which have not, except during wartime, conscripted citizens into their armed forces. It has always had a small standing army, thanks to the security afforded by powerful allies like Britain and, more recently, the United States. Nevertheless, Canada's response to the two world wars was immediate, and our contribution was truly remarkable. For a thinly populated nation, Canada made a human sacrifice of extraordinary size.

In this book, we will examine the Canadian contribution to the two world wars of this century. The impact of these wars on Canadian society at home is an important part of the story. War has affected all aspects of our society, women as well as men, civilians as well as soldiers. Indeed, in modern warfare, civilians are just as likely to suffer from the violence of war as soldiers are.

Canada is fortunate that it has not suffered the destruction of war on its own soil in this century. However, the world is now too small to pretend that this could never happen. We are all members of a global community. We all share the responsibility for its survival and for the welfare of its people. Unless we try to understand human conflict and are committed to finding alternatives to war, the sacrifice of all the millions who have died in past wars will have been in vain.

CHAPTER ONE

The Nature of War

War is an open conflict of arms between hostile parties or nations. Since the beginning of recorded history, we have had family or clan wars, tribal wars, civil wars, revolutionary wars, and international wars. Today we have guerrilla wars and gang wars. War is a form of fighting that involves weapons, organization, obedience to leaders, and usually commitment to a particular nation or cause.

War and fighting are violent attempts to get or hang onto something, to defend something, or to resolve some conflict. People resort to war when they feel unable to give up whatever it is they are after and when peaceful attempts have not been tried or have not worked. Wars and fights result from a combination of wanting something and of being unwilling or unable to get it peaceably.

Wars have been started for self-defence, freedom, food, land, money, honour, glory, power, revenge, and other things people have desired to get or to hold onto. When people want these things enough and are frustrated in peaceful attempts to get or hold onto them, they become willing to go to war — to kill or risk being killed.

Have you ever been in a fight? If so, what were you trying to accomplish? Do you think you could have prevented the fight by giving up what you wanted? Do you think you could have gotten what you wanted by peaceful means? Or do you think that fighting was the only way to resolve the conflict? Was the conflict satisfactorily resolved? If you were faced with the same situation again, would you act in the same way?

Why have civilized people allowed wars to take place? Why are nations and groups of people within nations using violence, instead of reason, in trying to resolve disagreements? Why do we continue to treat one another so brutally?

Peace rules the day where reason rules the mind.

William Collins

If a visitor arrived from another planet and reviewed our history in this century, he would certainly conclude that human beings are suicidal. This apparent self-destructive side of human nature has led many to believe that we are naturally violent and destructive. They feel that therefore wars are inevitable. Many philosophers and psychologists have agreed with this.

Others believe we are conditioned by our families, friends, education, and society. They say that we fight wars because we have seen war as an acceptable, and even necessary, method of getting what we want. We fight because we have not learned to have the patience we would need to use peaceful methods in resolving conflicts. Conflict is perhaps inevitable, they say, but war certainly is not.

Why Do Nations Start Wars?

In early times, a very few powerful persons could usually be blamed for starting wars. Their reasons were often quite personal — ambition to expand an empire, greed for treasures from other countries, religious fervor or fanaticism, and so on. Rulers often hired armies of mercenaries to fight these more or less personal wars for them.

In the twentieth century, wars have generally begun for more complex reasons. And most nations today, including the democracies, expect their own citizens willingly to give their lives in time of war.

Often there are many causes for the outbreak of a war. There may be long-standing international rivalries in addition to other causes such as economic interests, military ambition,

and national defence. These can result in a tangled web of conflicting national interests which can plunge several nations into war at one time. When we look at the First World War, we see that it began for relatively small reasons and eventually came near to wiping out a whole generation of young people, changing European society forever.

When individuals fight with one another, they are subject to laws which punish violence and inhumane conduct. In world affairs, however, it is quite different. Nations have agreements banning certain methods of warfare and calling for the humane treatment of prisoners. But they cannot easily be punished for breaking these agreements as a person can be punished in the law courts. Therefore they often act against other nations in ways that would be forbidden to their own citizens at home. From time to time, most recently in the Second World War and in Vietnam, the mass destruction of civilian populations has been condoned by political and military leaders. There are very few, if any, "fair wars" where everybody obeys the rules.

Nations have had perhaps three major causes for going to war in the twentieth century: (1) power rivalries, (2) expansion or protection of resources, and (3) nationalism. However, there has seldom been a single, clear-cut cause of war; wars have usually arisen out of a combination of causes.

Power Rivalries

Rivalries among the great powers of Europe can be traced back at least as far as to their colonial rivalries in Africa in the 1880s. Since 1815, the European nations had been held in check by a balance of power in Europe. However, growing international tensions finally reached the breaking point in 1914. After a long series of international incidents, the assassination of the heir to the Austro-Hungarian Empire was the final straw. This incident, along with the massive build-up of arms and the enthusiasm for military solutions to international problems, plunged Europe into the First World War.

Expansion or Protection of Resources

A major cause of international conflict has always been the desire to gain more land, more living space, more food and other resources. As populations have increased, countries have become crowded. Food and space then become uncomfortably limited. Europe has, of course, suffered much more than North America in this respect.

Between the seventeenth and twentieth centuries, no war was fought specifically for the expansion of land. Then, in the 1930s, Adolf Hitler justified his aggressive foreign policies by saying he had to have *"Lebensraum,"* or living space, for the German population. He invaded Czechoslovakia, Austria, and Poland to get this extra living space. The Japanese began aggression to build up a greater Southeast Asia. The Italians dreamed of acquiring a New Roman Empire. These made the Second World War a classic example of waging war for territorial and economic gain.

Some wars indirectly aim at the protection of resources and economic advantages by attempting to maintain international stability. The great rival powers have often become involved in "limited" wars, intervening with direct military assistance or with other forms of support in the wars and disputes of smaller countries. By maintaining stability in these countries, the larger powers can protect their own economic interests.

The gigantic multinational corporations of large nations have many billions of dollars invested in other countries. The parent nations of these corporations are concerned with protecting these investments and having free access to them. These financial interests have now become a big factor in modern foreign relations and military plans and alliances. The need for international stability, to prevent nations from going to war over these interests, is now greater than ever before.

Nationalism

Much warfare has owed its beginning to nationalism — the conviction that national interests are more important than anything else. Many wars have been fought, and are now being fought, to establish nations and promote a national identity. Nations which have already become established in history have often fought to make themselves greater, more powerful, and more glorious. Nationalism has even driven some countries to fight just for revenge or for conquests to boast of.

Nationalism often encourages the belief that the original citizens of one nation are actually better people than later immigrants or citizens of other countries. This belief in national superiority had especially evil results in Nazi Germany during the Second World War.

Religious traditions also feed into nationalism, as can be seen with India and Pakistan, Lebanon, and the Arab-Israeli wars. Tribal wars are similarly nationalistic in character. Self-assertion is the underlying factor in nationalism.

Why Do Soldiers Go to War?

However complex the reasons may be, the decisions that take nations into war are made by a rather small handful of leaders. The leaders may or may not represent the will of the people at large. Nevertheless, they are the ones who actually start the wars. But if wars are begun by a few individuals, they are fought by millions.

What makes soldiers leave their families, not knowing when or whether they will ever return? Men and women who go to war leave heartbreak and loneliness behind them. What kind of force can cause them to leave their homes to fight in a foreign land? Even if they are lucky enough to return, will it be without some lifelong disability? Is anyone really uninjured by warfare? Soldiers can be injured for the rest of their lives by the pictures that remain in their minds — pictures of fallen comrades, of dealing in death. The memories of war can make the pain of war linger for many years.

Few people who have experienced war at first hand will welcome another. Even today, Canadian veterans of the First World War do not like to talk of the carnage and widespread slaughter of that war. General Dwight Eisenhower, the American Commander-in-Chief of the Second World War, once exclaimed, "I hate war as only a soldier who has lived with it can, only as one who has seen its brutality, its futility, its stupidity."

Why, then, are men and women willing to fight? No matter what reasons governments may have for waging wars, individuals have a variety of personal reasons for volunteering to fight. A person's reasons may have little to do with the reasons of the government. Personal reasons might be broken down into four main areas: (1) self-defence, (2) patriotism, (3) the excitement of war, and (4) the sense of companionship that war can create. We will look into each of these reasons as they are expressed in the prose and poetry of the soldiers themselves.

The Send-Off

Wilfred Owen (1893-1918)

Down the close, darkening lanes they sang their way
To the siding-shed,
And lined the train with faces grimly gay,
Their breasts were stuck all white with wreath and spray
As men's are, dead.

Dull porters watched them, and a casual tramp
Stood staring hard,
Sorry to miss them from the upland camp.
Then, unmoved, signals nodded, and a lamp
Winked to the guard.

So secretly, like wrongs hushed up, they went.
They were not ours:
We never heard to which front these were sent.
Nor there if they yet mock what women meant
Who gave them flowers.

Shall they return to beatings of great bells
In wild trainloads?
A few, a few, too few for drums and yells,
May creep back, silent, to village wells
Up half-known roads.

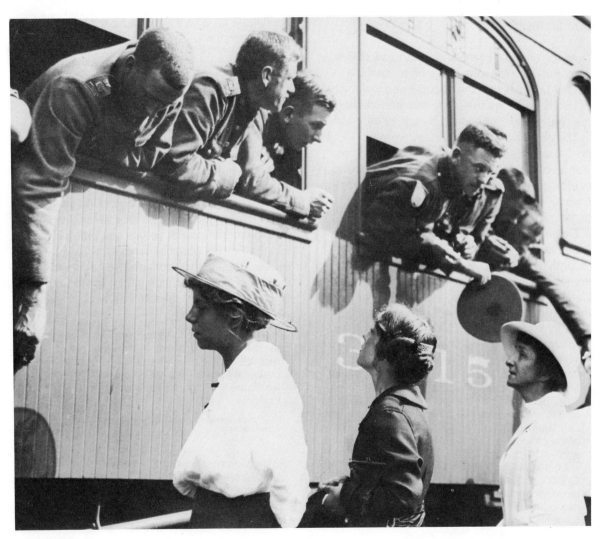

Departure

City of Toronto Archives, James Collection

Inevitably came the time of parting. Embarkation leave ended in kisses and tears and many brave smiles — and a little boy's hand reaching for one last precious moment in his dad's. The troop train began to move. The soldier drew his wife to him again. Their kiss, ineffably soft and gentle, seemed to fuse them. Then he turned and sprang on the last car. The train was crowded with faces, and he was one of them, but she could not see him. She stood for a long time on the platform, her eyes fixed on the trail of smoke against the sky. Gradually there stole over her the sensation that the flame of her life had left her and she was only a shell. She felt cold and empty. When she got home, she sat for a long time listening to the silence of the room. — *Edward Meade*

Self-Defence

Defence of one's homeland is certainly the most powerful of all reasons for going to war. If a soldier believes that the security and well-being of family and community are threatened, then the reasons for fighting will be purely defensive.

The great wars of this century were not fought on Canadian soil. Nonetheless, many still saw war as being defensive, because losing the overseas war could be a disaster for the whole Empire and threaten the safety of all the democratic nations.

Defence motivated a majority of the British Canadians in 1914. Many of them had only recently immigrated to Canada. They saw little immediate danger to Canada; but, for them, Canada's well-being was bound to that of the British Empire. A typical view is expressed by Jane Walters, a nurse from a small Ontario town who served in the First World War:

We were British Canadians. That speaks for itself. My people were all British, all English. In those days, patriotism was rife. You didn't think about the cost to yourself, you just did it when it was needed. Our family did it, and so, I suppose, did the families of the other girls. That's why they had the same spirit.

England called. Most of us were British Canadians: Canadians first, British second. But we never thought of separating them. My father used to say to me, "My dear, be proud you're English, and remember: Honour first." So that was my picture of an English person — "Honour first."

We didn't understand the causes of the war. We just knew England was in danger. We couldn't understand it, we hadn't time to think about it. It was only later, as we got a little older and read more, that we learned about all the underlying causes of war. But even if we had, what would that have mattered? England was in danger. Canadian men were going over, and if Canadian women got a chance to go, they should go and help.

As quoted in Daphne Read, Ed., *The Great War and Canadian Society* (Toronto: New Hogtown Press, 1978)

Men and women often fight for the defence of universal human rights as well as for the defence of their own lives and well-being. This was especially true in the Second World War, when fascist governments took away the freedom of millions of people and plunged them into the horrors of racial genocide. Many believed that if such forces were not stopped, the rights of Canadians might at some future time be seriously threatened as well.

We are fighting in a war for justice, for honour, and for liberty. We in Canada . . . have no selfish motives and no desire for profit. . . . We are fighting, or will be fighting, against policies and principles which are anti-Christian and anti-democratic . . . barbarous and brutal.

R.J. Manion (Conservative Party), House of Commons Debates, September, 1939

The Co-operative Commonwealth Federation recognizes that Canada is now implicated in a struggle which may involve the survival of democratic institutions. . . . Canada should be prepared to defend her own shore, but her assistance overseas should be limited to economic aid and must not include conscription of manpower or the sending of any expeditionary force.

M.J. Coldwell (C.C.F. Party), House of Commons Debates, September, 1939

For what reasons, if any, would you go to war?

When a nation is at war, do its citizens have the right to oppose that war?

Once a soldier is in battle, the motive of self-defence becomes a powerful reason to fight. Each soldier is then fighting to stay alive. It is usually a matter of killing or being killed. When this motive of personal survival becomes uppermost, fighting troops easily fall into despair. After experiencing four years of the agony of trench warfare in France and Flanders in World War I, even the most idealistic soldiers became disillusioned.

A Disillusioned Soldier

I enlisted a few days after I was eighteen years old, in January, 1917. I must say that, looking back on it, I was completely brainwashed by the society in which I lived. I never questioned the total rightness of our cause. . . . I never questioned that what we were doing was right and that the Germans were all wrong and that we were fighting to make the world safe for democracy.

This attitude was not typical, as I found when I got into the army, of any but a small, idealistic group of students, of people who came from teachers' families or preachers' families. That was one of the first shocks to me.

We had a few fellows around who had been over, who had been wounded, and who were doing some of the training. And they were cynical and scornful — ''You'll get over that when you get over there'' — if you expressed any idealistic feeling about the war.

Keith Fallis, as quoted in Daphne Read, Ed., *The Great War and Canadian Society* (Toronto: New Hogtown Press, 1978)

Wartime Existence   *Public Archives Canada PA-2468*

Most of the soldier's life was spent in the wet, cold dugouts that zigzagged across the Western Front. While the rest of these Canadians try to sleep, one soldier takes advantage of a lull in the fighting to write a letter home.

As the First World War dragged on, some of the most disillusioned spoke out against the suffering of their fellow soldiers. One was Second-Lieutenant Siegfried Sassoon, a British officer who had already received the Military Cross for bravery and was recommended for the Distinguished Service Order. In July of 1917, he submitted the following statement to his commanding officer:

I am making this statement as an act of willful defiance of military authority, because I believe that the war is being deliberately prolonged by those who have the power to end it.

I am a soldier, convinced that I am acting on behalf of soldiers. I believe that this war, upon which I entered as a war of defence and liberation, has become a war of aggression and conquest. I believe that the purposes for which I and my fellow soldiers entered upon this war should have been so clearly stated as to have made it impossible to change them, and that, had this been done, the objects which activated us would now be attainable by negotiation.

I have seen and endured the sufferings of the troops, and I can no longer be a party to prolong these sufferings for the ends which I believe to be evil and unjust.

Sassoon went on to say that he was not complaining of the way in which the war was being conducted. He was protesting the insincerity of the political leaders and the callous complacency with which the people at home regarded "the continuation of agonies which they do not share."

Few soldiers went this far, although many sympathized with Sassoon's views. Keith Fallis expressed the attitude of many of the troops:

If the war is justified, then you have to accept all your responsibilities, you see. But I never went over to Siegfried Sassoon's position that, because of the nature of it, you have to repudiate it. But I think that because of that experience and also going over to the front and seeing men killed for the first time, and horses shot to pieces, I froze up.

I just wouldn't think about it. I just hung onto this: the best we could hope was that this war would make the world safe for democracy; and it's a helluva business, and the sooner we get it over with, the better.

As quoted in Daphne Read, Ed., *The Great War and Canadian Society* (Toronto: New Hogtown Press, 1978)

Patriotism

Loyalty and patriotism were especially strong motives for enlistment in the First World War. Soldiers believed they had a moral obligation to obey their national leaders, even to the point of sacrificing their own lifes.

The accompanying two poems illustrate the acceptance of self-sacrifice for one's country. "The Soldier" is by an English poet. The well-known "In Flanders Fields" is by a Canadian.

A young German soldier named Franz Blumenfeld expressed the same spirit of self-sacrifice. While on a troop train heading for the front lines on September 23, 1914, just after the outbreak of war, he wrote home to his parents:

I want to write to you about something else, which, judging from bits in your letters, you haven't quite understood: why I should have volunteered for the war? Of course it was not from any enthusiasm for war in general, nor because I thought it would be a fine thing to kill a great many people or otherwise distinguish myself. On the contrary, I think that war is a very, very evil thing, and I believe that even in this case it might have been averted by a more skilful diplomacy. But, now that it has been

Boredom makes me want to damage something or pick a fight. I think boredom makes a lot of people destructive.

A 14-Year-Old Student

The Soldier

Rupert Brooke (1887-1915)

If I should die, think only this for me
That there's some corner of a foreign field
That is forever England. There shall be
In that rich earth a richer dust concealed;
A dust whom England bore, shaped, made aware,
Gave, once, her flowers to love, her ways to roam,
A body of England's, breathing English air,
Washed by the rivers, blest by suns of home.

And think this heart, all evil shed away,
A pulse in the eternal mind, no less
Gives somewhere back the thoughts by England given;
Her sights and sounds; dreams happy as her day;
And laughter, learnt of friends; and gentleness,
In hearts at peace, under an English heaven.

In Flanders Fields

John McCrae (1872-1918)

In Flanders fields the poppies blow
Between the crosses, row on row,
That mark our place; and in the sky
The larks, still bravely singing, fly
Scarce heard amid the guns below.

We are the Dead. Short days ago
We lived, felt dawn, saw sunset glow,
Loved, and were loved, and now we lie
In Flanders fields.

Take up our quarrel with the foe;
To you from failing hands we throw
The torch; be yours to hold it high.
If ye break faith with us who die
We shall not sleep, though poppies grow
In Flanders fields.

declared, I think it is a matter of course that one should feel oneself so much a member of the nation that one must unite one's fate as closely as possible with that of the whole. . . . What counts is always the readiness to make a sacrifice, not the object for which the sacrifice is made.

This war seems to me, from all that I have heard, to be something so horrible, inhuman, mad, obsolete, and in every way depraving, that I have firmly resolved, if I do come back, to do everything in my power to prevent such a thing from ever happening again.

Franz Blumenfeld was killed before Christmas of 1914.

The Excitement of War

With war comes challenge, self-assertion, the prospect of victory, and the image of heroism. War is exciting, even with the risk of life and physical hardship. At the beginning of this century, the new technological society often made the average person's life rather boring. Many were caught in a daily routine that was lacking in adventure. War gave such people a chance to throw themselves into something more exciting. Few could resist the splended colours of the regiments, the blaring sounds of marching bands, the dream of glory and triumph over the enemy. Many enlisted just to experience the excitement of war.

War

Richard LeGalliene

War I abhor, and yet how sweet
The sound along the marching street
Of drum and fife, and I forget
Wet eyes of widows, and forget
Broken old mothers, and the whole
Dark butchery without a soul.

A man who experiences no genuine satisfaction in life does not want peace. . . . People court war to escape meaninglessness and boredom, to be relieved of fear and frustration.

Nels F.S. Ferre

Canada in 1914

Canada was still a rural country in 1914. In small towns and villages, young men readily joined up.

The Excitement of Enlisting

Why did I enlist? Well, my motives are mixed. I was only past my twenty-first birthday. The prospect of adventure and travel and so on had a very strong appeal for me. I would say I had other reasons for it too. My reading was almost entirely based on *Boy's Own Annual* and *Chums* and Henty and so on. So I had the belief that Britain always won its wars and that they were always right. This was a feeling that my generation had. . . .

I think most people joined from a sense of perhaps duty and desire for a change perhaps — you know, occupation, excitement, adventure. I think I would put the emphasis on the fact that most of us were young and saw it as a wonderful opportunity to throw off the shackles of working in an office or a factory or on a farm or what-have-you. — *Larry Nelson*

When the war broke out — you cannot believe unless you were there. The country went mad! People were singing on the streets and roads. Everybody wanted to be a hero, everybody wanted to go to war. Hadn't had a war since the Boer War in 1899, 1900, which I remember. There was nothing between that in wars, and everybody was going to be a hero, and I wanted to be a hero too. But I wasn't big enough. I was only five foot nothing and weighed 85 pounds and was a Boy Scout bugler. I remember walking up Park Avenue in Montreal blowing the bugle, everybody was excited, the war was on. — *Bert Remington*

As quoted in Daphne Read, Ed., *The Great War and Canadian Society* (Toronto: New Hogtown Press, 1978)

In the following excerpt, Walter Limmer, a young German soldier, writes to his parents just after his enlistment in August, 1914. Within two months after writing this letter, he was dead.

[The] night when England's declaration of war was announced in the barracks . . . none of us got to sleep till three o'clock in the morning, we were so full of excitement, fury, and enthusiasm. It is a joy to go to the Front with such comrades. We are bound to be victorious! Nothing else is possible in the face of such determination to win. My dear ones, be proud that you live in such times and in such a nation, and that you too have the privilege of sending several of those you love into this glorious struggle. . . .

This hour is one such as seldom strikes in the life of a nation, and it is so marvellous and moving as to be in itself sufficient compensation for many sufferings and sacrifices.

Metropolitan Toronto Library Board

A Second World War Recruiting Poster

Why is war exciting for some people? Is it ever exciting for the fighting soldier?

Why do you think the feeling of fellowship is so strong among soldiers in wartime?

Many were excited about the war only because it promised them a job and some security. Others saw it as an opportunity to escape from dull work and meagre pay.

Surprisingly, there was a lot of unemployment in 1913 and 1914. There was a depression as far as employment was concerned, and there were thousands of unemployed people who were happy to join the army. They were dressed properly, they got their meals, their training camps. They enjoyed themselves. They had some purpose in living. So thousands joined the army because of economic circumstances. — *Sam Beckman*

When the war broke out, I run away from the home I was in, Fagan's Homes. I run away and joined the army, and I gave me age as eighteen. I was between fourteen and fifteen. I didn't wash or anything or shine my shoes or clean anything. I looked just tough, you know, like a regular farm boy. I joined the army and I went in as a sniper.

The average young fella was running away, you know. Things are different now. You see, I was only getting five dollars a year and my keep. When I joined the army I was getting more — $1.10 a day. — *Burt Woods*

As quoted in Daphne Read, Ed., *The Great War and Canadian Society* (Toronto: New Hogtown Press, 1978)

In the end, the young people who went to war for the excitement of it were just as disillusioned as those who had enlisted out of patriotism or other motives. A German soldier, Sven Hassel, wrote of his disillusionment in the First World War:

Only a few find war exciting and romantic. To most, it is dirt, suffering, endless monotony. . . . War is a bad way of experiencing the heights of life; it leaves you disappointed, and when you come back from it, you discover that you . . . have lost contact with that to which you have returned.

Companionship in War

War gives soldiers an unusual dependence upon one another and a great closeness to one another. Soldiers say that in war you see more honesty, comradeship, generosity, and self-sacrifice for others than you ever see in times of peace. War creates a common bond. Everyone is on the same side. Class and economic inequalities often disappear. Some people have said that if civilian life could provide the comradeship, equality, and idealism that are found in war, it might be very difficult to get volunteers to fight a war.

When soldiers talk of war, the companionship is what they most often recall. Friendships sealed in war have frequently lasted a lifetime. Old "comrades-in-arms" like to maintain their associations long after war is over because of the rich quality of their wartime friendships. Legion halls across Canada are full of stories of friendships between men and women who have shown great courage and sacrifice for others.

The feeling of a common bond, of respect and sympathy, quite often extended to the enemy as well as to a soldier's own comrades. A Newfoundlander who enlisted in 1915 had this to say about his attitude toward the German soldiers:

It seemed that they didn't want to be there any more than we did. But it seemed that somebody else was manipulating the strings behind the line, and we were just put there to work out a game.

It wasn't really hatred. Only sometimes you did hate, when you'd see your chums and your friends get shot. It would be pretty hard on you that way, and you could say you'd hate for awhile, but not necessarily hate that you wanted to kill. But you had to kill or be killed, if you wanted to survive. Sometimes you'd think of all the killing, how unnecessary it was when you could live in peace with each other till somebody stirred up a lot of

The world will never have lasting peace as long as men reserve for war the finest human qualities.

John Foster Dulles (U.S. Secretary of State)

Fraternization at the Front: Christmas Day, 1914

The feeling of fellowship, born of common suffering, has sometimes spilled across the front lines to include enemy soldiers as well as our own. This has happened in both world wars. The best-known example was the fraternization between German and British troops on Christmas Day, 1914.

By this time, the war had already bogged down in the trenches. Little did the troops on either side know that it was to last four more terrible years. The following account by Frank Richards, a British private, describes one of the many similar incidences that took place all along the Western Front:

On Christmas morning, we stuck up a board with "A Merry Christmas" on it. The enemy had stuck up a similar one. . . . Two of our men then threw their equipment off and jumped on the parapet with their hands above their heads. Two of the Germans did the same and commenced to walk up the riverbank, our two men going to meet them. They met and shook hands, and then we all got out of the trench. . . . We and the Germans met in the middle of no-man's-land. Their officers were also now out. Our officers exchanged greetings with them. One of the German officers said that he wished he had a camera to take a snapshot, but they were not allowed to carry cameras. Neither were our officers.

We mucked in all day with one another. . . . By the look of them, their trenches were in as bad a state as our own. One of their men, speaking English, mentioned that he had worked in Brighton for some years and that he was fed up to the neck with this damned war and would be glad when it was all over. We told him that he wasn't the only one that was fed up with it. . . .

The German company commander asked our commander if he would accept a couple of barrels of beer and assured him that they would not make his men drunk. They had plenty of it in the brewery. He accepted the offer with thanks, and a couple of their men rolled the barrels over, and we took them into our trench. The German officer sent one of his men back to the trench, who appeared shortly after carrying a tray with bottles and glasses on it. Officers of both sides clinked glasses and drank one another's health. Our commander had presented them with a plum pudding just before. The officers came to an understanding that the unofficial truce would end at midnight. At dusk we went back to our respective trenches. . . .

During this time we often carried on conversations with the enemy. . . . We were never opposite a German regiment during this time but what didn't have a few men who could speak English. In one German regiment they had a wonderful violin player who often played selections from operas, and in the summer evenings, when a slight breeze was blowing towards us, we could distinguish every note. We always gave him a clap and shouted for an encore.

hatred and then got you into this fighting that you had no part of really. They seemed to be playing a game of this.

Sometimes at that time there, I felt, well, it's so unnecessary. A bunch of men, say a hundred and fifty yards or a hundred yards away — you could talk to them and you could hear them talking, hear them working, and here you were, you got to make an attack. And you had to kill them or get killed. And you would sometimes wonder what it was all about.

As quoted in Daphne Read, Ed., *The Great War and Canadian Society* (Toronto: New Hogtown Press, 1978)

The Universal Soldier

Buffy Sainte-Marie

He's five foot two and he's six feet four,
  he fights with missiles and with spears,
He's all of thirty-one and he's only seventeen,
  he's been a soldier for a thousand years.

He's a Catholic, a Hindu, an Atheist, a Jain,
  a Buddhist and a Baptist and a Jew,
And he knows he shouldn't kill and he knows he always will
  kill you for me, my friend, and me for you;

And he's fighting for Canada, he's fighting for France,
  he's fighting for the U.S.A.,
And he's fighting for the Russians and he's fighting for Japan,
  and he thinks we'll put an end to war that way.

And he's fighting for democracy, he's fighting for the Reds,
  he says it's for the peace of all,
He's the one who must decide who's to live and who's to die,
  and he never sees the writing on the wall.

But without him how would Hitler have condemned him at Dachau,
  without him Caesar would have stood alone.
He's the one who gives his body as a weapon of the war,
  and without him all this killing can't go on.

He's the Universal Soldier and he really is to blame,
  his orders come from far away no more,
They come from him and you and me, and, brothers can't you see,
  This is not the way we put an end to war.

Young German Soldiers Captured by Canadians during the First World War

*Never think that war, no matter how necessary nor how justified, is
not a crime.*

Ernest Hemingway

Public Archives Canada PA-1107

Summary

Nations and groups within nations start wars for various reasons. The main causes of wars between nations are: international rivalries among the great powers, expansion or protection of resources, and nationalism. The decision to go to war is made by a comparatively few persons, who may or may not represent the will of the citizens at large in a country. Although wars are caused by a few leaders, they are fought by millions; and many millions suffer because of war.

Individuals join in a war for various personal reasons. Their chief reasons are: self-defence, patriotism, the excitement of war, and the comradeship they find in war. Disillusionment is a common result of going to war.

In the next chapter, we will try to see what war was like for the Canadians who participated in the two world wars of this century.

CHAPTER TWO

Canada and the First World War

In Chapter One, we discussed why nations go to war and what causes people to fight. The Great War (or, as it later came to be called, the First World War) is perhaps the best example of how a mixture of national ambitions, power rivalries, and foolish leadership can take nations to war.

For a majority of Europeans, the beginning of the twentieth century was a true blossoming of western civilization. Except for some brief wars limited to a few nations, Europe had known a century of relative calm. For more than forty years, no war had taken place on European soil. Yet the seeds of war were being methodically sown as rival empires vied for national expansion, imperial wealth, and military power.

Europe in 1914 was, in many ways, a unified civilization. A person could travel across borders without worrying about a passport. An individual could even settle in another country without restrictions or government interference. Most nations were run by limited monarchies; the only republics at that time were France and Portugal. Everything seemed serene and calm. But in August, 1914, war came to Europe like a lightning bolt out of the blue summer skies. What had happened?

Public Archives Canada PA-3778

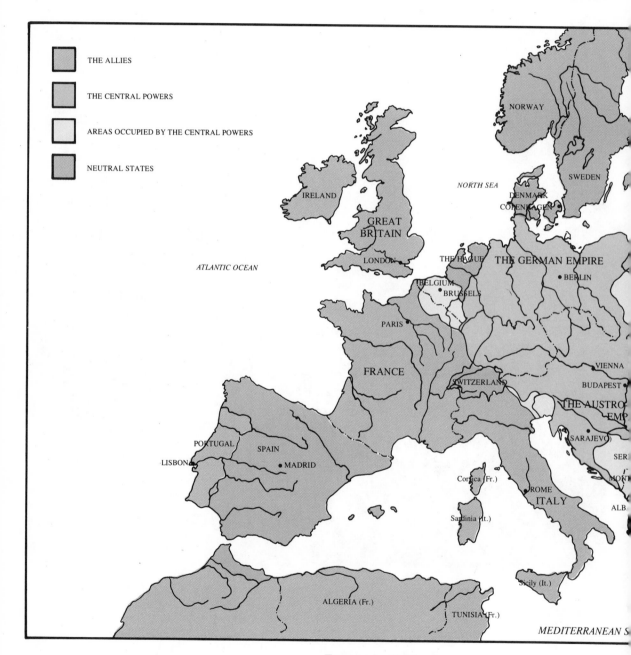

Europe in 1914

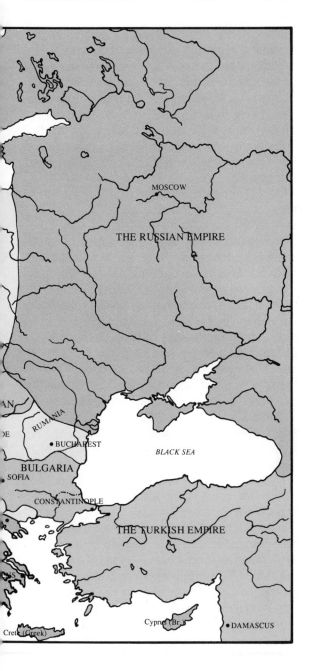

On June 28, 1914, Grand Duke Franz Ferdinand, the popular heir to the Austro-Hungarian Empire, and his wife were assassinated while on a state visit to Sarajevo in the Austrian province of Bosnia. The assassin was Gavrilo Princip, a Bosnian. It was suspected that he was backed by the Serbian secret police. Events moved quickly. The world was shocked by the murders. People generally wanted some punishment of Serbia.

Austria sent an ultimatum to Serbia. It demanded, among other things, Serbian assistance in stamping out the terrorist group responsible for the murders. The German government supported Austria in its demands. Germany's support has often been called a "blank cheque," because it promised to support whatever Austria decided to do. This turned out to be a serious mistake.

Serbia's existence as an independent nation was at stake. It accepted all but two of the terms of the ultimatum. But Austria declared war on Serbia anyway. This was because Serbia was attempting to unite the Slavic minorities of the Austro-Hungarian Empire into an independent nation. Austria saw these attempts as a continuing threat to the peace of the Empire. The Serbs must be taught a lesson.

In support of Serbia, Tsar Nicholas II ordered the huge Russian army to prepare for war. Once these preparations began, they were not easy to stop. Germany asked Russia to stop its mobilization. It refused, and Germany declared war.

France, which was allied with Russia, immediately began to mobilize as well. Many French military leaders welcomed the possibility of war with Germany. It would provide them with an opportunity to get revenge for their defeat by Prussia some forty years earlier. Some German military leaders also welcomed the prospect of war with France.

Germany, frightened by the mobilization of Russia's monstrous army, decided it had to act swiftly. The German *"Schlieffen* Plan" called for a lightning strike by most of the army against Paris. It was expected that this would defeat France within six weeks. Unless they acted before Russia's immense army was fully mobilized, the Germans would have to fight a war on two fronts. Believing that the British would stay out, Germany declared war on France.

Germany attacked France by going through Belgium on August 4, 1914, and Britain had guaranteed Belgian neutrality. Britain therefore declared war on Germany. Thus a conflict that had begun a month earlier with pistol shots in a small Balkan town led Europe into the most devastating conflict of its history. By the end of the Great War, forty million people would be dead, thirty million of them civilians.

The British Empire Declares War

At eleven o'clock in the evening of August 4, 1914 (midnight in Berlin), the British government handed the German ambassador in London a declaration of war. Earlier that day, Germany's elite Uhlans Cavalry had crossed the frontier of Belgium. In so doing, Germany had violated the long-standing British treaty with Belgium which guaranteed Belgian neutrality. By midnight of that same day, Britain's declaration of war had brought the entire British Empire into the conflict.

In 1914, the Empire was the greatest the world had ever known, greater even than that of the Romans or the Mongols. It covered a quarter of the earth's land surface, and its influence reached everywhere. Canada, Australia, New Zealand, India, and South Africa were all parts of this vast company of nations and cultures.

Without the Empire's support, Britain's success in a war against the superior forces of Germany would have been far less certain. The Royal Navy "ruled the waves." However, the manpower, surplus food, and economic wealth of the dominions would prove to be essential for maintaining the Allied war effort during the next four years.

Most Europeans expected little contribution from countries like Canada and Australia, who were far removed from the European quarrel. Many felt that these distant colonies would show little loyalty. However, the size and swiftness of the imperial response astonished all of Europe and amazed even the British leaders.

The colonies and former colonies prepared for war with incredible speed. Except for India, none had a large regular army. In August of 1914, Canada had a permanent force of only 3110 men. Nevertheless, within two months of the outbreak of war, Canada armed 30 000 men and sent them to Britain in a great flotilla of 32 ships.

By the start of the war, Canada was responsible for its own naval defence. In 1910, Britain had turned over the old naval bases of Halifax and Esquimalt to Canada. Subsequently, the Naval Bill was passed by the Canadian Parliament, establishing a separate Canadian naval service.

In 1910, Canada purchased two old cruisers from Britain, to be used as training ships. In 1914, however, both ships — H.M.C.S. *Niobe* and H.M.C.S. *Rainbow* — were pressed into service for naval operations. By the end of the First World War, about 5000 Canadians had been recruited for naval service; some 1500 of them served on British warships. After 1917, Canadian naval trawlers carried out anti-submarine patrols in the North Atlantic. However, the Royal Canadian Navy was still a small force with a rather precarious future in 1918.

At the start of the First World War, Canada had a regular army of only 3110 soldiers and 684 horses. There was a reserve militia, which provided enthusiastic amateur soldiers with, on the average, four days of field training a year. One Canadian army officer described the reserve as "the most expensive and ineffective military system of any civilized country in the world."

And yet, by 1918, a full-time fighting force of 100 000 soldiers, led by Canadian generals, had won a combat reputation second to none. By the end of the war in November, 1918, a total of 619 636 Canadian men and women had served in the Canadian Expeditionary Force. Of this number, 59 544 never returned and 172 950 were wounded.

Canada's contribution to the "Great War" was a remarkable achievement for a population of fewer than eight million. Since Confederation, Canada had only once before officially sent troops abroad to fight for the British Empire. In 1899, Prime Minister Wilfrid Laurier had allowed several contingents of Canadian volunteers to be sent to South Africa to help the British subdue the Boer republics. A total of 7368 Canadians had served with the British forces between 1899 and 1902.

The Royal Canadian Regiment and the First Gordon Highlanders Crossing the Modder River at the Start of the Battle for Paardeberg in the South African War, February 18, 1900

Canadians Join the War

In the summer of 1914, a great many Canadians were on their holidays, enjoying long, lazy, sunny days by rivers and lakes. Canada had nothing to do with the complex events in Europe. Few Canadians noticed the approach of war. Nevertheless, the moment Britain declared war, Canada was at war as well. Before 1914, most English Canadians still saw themselves as British subjects living in an overseas colony. When war came, their response was immediate. Thousands quickly rallied to the colours. One young man who volunteered recalled later on:

> I was in a moving picture show in Yorkton, Saskatchewan, on the fourth of August, and it flashed up on the screen that Germany had declared war on England. So a young Welshman and I, as soon as the show was over, we went over to the local unit of the 16th Light Horse and told them that the war was on and we wanted to enlist. The major in charge, he hadn't heard about it, but he got a sheet of foolscap out and headed it up "Enlistments for the German War," and we put our names down.

Throughout Canada, armories were besieged by mobs of young men, all eager to enlist. A British Columbia youth wrote:

> I was 27. I was one of the original 88th Fusiliers which started in Victoria. And then we were called up suddenly and they asked us, those who wished to join up to go overseas step forward, and the whole battalion stepped forward.

Colonel Sam Hughes, a Lindsay, Ontario, newspaperman, had become Minister of Militia and Defence in 1911. His enormous vitality resulted in an amazing recruiting effort, mustering over 30 000 volunteers at a training camp at Valcartier, on the outskirts of Quebec City. In early October, 1914, the First Division of the Canadian Expeditionary Force was heading across the Atlantic for Britain, escorted by ten warships. They arrived in Plymouth, England, on October 14.

The Canadians were disappointed to find that they had to spend a long, cold, wet winter in a tent camp on the Salisbury Plain. Lord Kitchener, the British Minister of War, had not been too impressed by the Canadian forces when they arrived in England. This led to a heated exchange between Kitchener and our tough Minister of Defence, Sir Sam Hughes. A Canadian officer who was present reported:

> Sir Sam marched up to Kitchener's desk. When he arrived at the desk, Kitchener spoke up quickly and in in a very stern voice said: "Hughes, I see you have brought over a number of men from Canada; they are of course without training, and this would apply to their officers. I have decided to divide them up among the British regiments; they will be of very little use to us as they are."
> Sir Sam replied: "Sir, do I understand you to say that you are going to break up these Canadian regiments that came over? Why, it will kill recruiting in Canada." Kitchener answered: "You have your orders; carry them out." Sir Sam replied: "I'll be damned if I will," turned on his heel, and marched out.

Hughes had his way. Canadian forces were to fight as a unit in the war. The first winter, spent on Salisbury Plain in England, was one of great discomfort. By Christmas of 1914, one experienced Canadian detachment, the Princess Patricia's Canadian Light Infantry, had already reached France. The Canadian division crossed to France in February of 1915. They and the other 400 000 Canadians who followed them were to distinguish themselves for their ability and courage.

When the troops first volunteered, many had done so promising their loved ones they would return within the year. Little did they know, in

Why was Canada's contribution to the First World War such a remarkable achievement?

What was the general reaction of Canadians to the outbreak of war in August, 1914?

"The Olympic," by Arthur Lismer

National Gallery of Canada

During the First World War, this famous ship carried 70 000 Canadian troops across the Atlantic to the United Kingdom. The "dazzle paint" broke up its outline and helped to conceal it from enemy submarines.

Why does "trench warfare" cause opposing armies to become bogged down?

Do you think the use of gas was justified? Are there weapons that should never be used in warfare?

those early months, that the war on the Western Front would soon bog down into years of stationary warfare with neither side gaining any real advantage. Each new attempt to break through the enemy lines would turn into a mass slaughter. Men were ordered by the tens of thousands to advance straight into enemy machine-gun fire and through an incredible mass of mud and barbed wire.

It was during this first foreign experience that Canadians began to earn their overseas reputation for raw courage. Canadian troops also became known for their breezy disregard for rank. Their relaxed attitudes toward rank and discipline contrasted with the regimentation of the more class-conscious British army. A cartoon appeared about them in the popular British magazine *Punch.* In it, a Canadian officer instructs his men, "And now, boys, we are to be inspected by an English general. And while he is here, be careful not to call me 'Alf.'"

Canada on the Western Front

By the time the Canadians arrived in France in early 1915, the war had become hopelessly bogged down along a long line which stretched unbroken from the North Sea to neutral Switzerland. A new kind of warfare began, for which no country had been prepared.

Enemy and allied trenches zigzagged along the entire Front. For four years, soldiers in these sandbagged and defensively wired trenches forced one another back and forth across a devastated no-man's land. Trenches were so close together that voices of the enemy soldiers could be heard clearly. Advances came only with

a terrible loss in lives, and they were measured in metres rather than kilometres.

Some important engagements of the war were fought in Africa and in the Middle East. But the Canadian army was to serve on the Western Front, where most of the decisive battles took place. The Newfoundland Regiment served with the British in the Dardanelles, but it returned to the Western Front in 1915.

Gas Attack at Ypres

The Canadian soldiers' first real contact with the grim realities of this war came in the historic Belgian city of Ypres. This region was considered an important objective by the Germans, as it was the last part of Belgium not yet occupied. The Canadians' First Division marched into the trenches outside Ypres early in April of 1915. It was here that they received their baptism of fire in battle.

On the evening of April 22, the Germans released the contents of 5730 cylinders of deadly chlorine gas. It drifted on an evening breeze towards the Allied trenches. The gas, which had never before been used in war, caused the sudden collapse of 6.5 km of Allied defences. The Algerians, who were holding the line to the left of the Canadians, retreated in panic from the suffocating, sickening fumes. Their eyes were blinded and their lungs choked.

The Germans were not fully prepared to exploit their powerful new weapon, and they did not advance as quickly as they might have to take advantage of the breakthrough. Working furiously throughout the night and the following day, the Canadians fought to close the huge gap in the front lines. On the following day, gas was released again. This time, it came directly at the

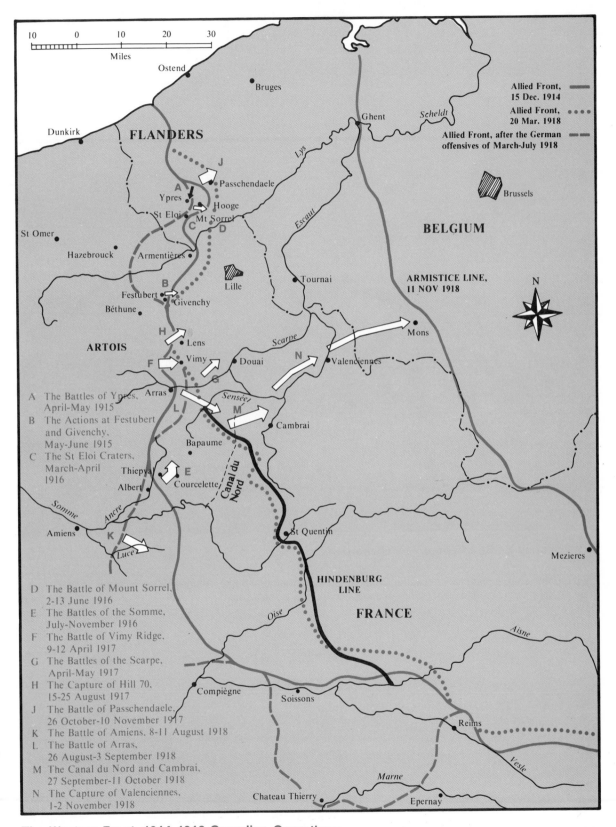

Map legend and labels:

Allied Front, 15 Dec. 1914
Allied Front, 20 Mar. 1918
Allied Front, after the German offensives of March-July 1918

ARMISTICE LINE, 11 NOV 1918

HINDENBURG LINE

FLANDERS

BELGIUM

ARTOIS

FRANCE

N

Place labels: Ostend, Bruges, Ghent, Scheldt, Dunkirk, Brussels, Lys, Escaut, Passchendaele, Ypres, Hooge, St Eloi, Mt Sorrel, St Omer, Hazebrouck, Armentières, Lille, Tournai, Festubert, Givenchy, Béthune, Lens, Scarpe, Mons, Vimy, Douai, Valenciennes, Arras, Sensée, Cambrai, Bapaume, Canal du Nord, Thiepval, Albert, Courcelette, Somme, Ancre, Amiens, Luce, St Quentin, Mezieres, Oise, Aisne, Compiègne, Soissons, Reims, Vesle, Marne, Chateau Thierry, Epernay

A The Battles of Ypres, April-May 1915
B The Actions at Festubert and Givenchy, May-June 1915
C The St Eloi Craters, March-April 1916
D The Battle of Mount Sorrel, 2-13 June 1916
E The Battles of the Somme, July-November 1916
F The Battle of Vimy Ridge, 9-12 April 1917
G The Battles of the Scarpe, April-May 1917
H The Capture of Hill 70, 15-25 August 1917
J The Battle of Passchendaele, 26 October-10 November 1917
K The Battle of Amiens, 8-11 August 1918
L The Battle of Arras, 26 August-3 September 1918
M The Canal du Nord and Cambrai, 27 September-11 October 1918
N The Capture of Valenciennes, 1-2 November 1918

10 0 10 20 30
Miles

The Western Front, 1914-1918 Canadian Operations

37

"The Second Battle of Ypres," by Richard Jack

National Gallery of Canada

Two months after arriving in France, the Canadians fought their first battle. Although they suffered heavily, they made a heroic stand against a horrible new weapon — poison gas.

Canadians. Despite tremendous losses from the gas and repeated German attacks, the Canadians stubbornly held their ground. A Canadian officer, amazed at the performance of his men, wrote:

I've never seen such marvellous men in all my life. They adjusted themselves to anything. It would be difficult to pick out any man for bravery, because they were all brave. I expected to see panic. There was no thought of panic. There was a job coming along and they just knuckled down to it, and really they were marvellous.

The battle of Ypres lasted three more weeks. In spite of heavy casualties, Ypres never fell. But even though it was never occupied, it was completely destroyed by the continuous enemy bombardment.

The Slaughter Continues (1915-1916)

Throughout the rest of 1915, the Allies repeatedly tried to break the deadlock on the Western Front. They soon found that offensives taken against such strong German defences were hopeless and caused a terrible loss of life. The shocking thing was that the British and French generals continued to order such foolish attacks in spite of incredible loss of life. John Swettenham, a Canadian military historian, describes "the stupidity of trying to win the war" through "wearing down" the enemy in this costly way:

The pathetic bodies in no-man's land were to little purpose: men died striving for a breakthrough that was unattainable with the equipment and the tactics available. The over-optimistic Allied generals, who saw only the unspoiled fields beyond and not the impregnability of the defensive lines — and who still hurled men forward in one useless attack after another — must be held to blame.

The French commander, Joffre — a short, fat man with a large mustache — was not discouraged by the results of the offensives he had planned. He was satisfied that "nibbling" would achieve results in time and closed his eyes to the enormous casualties:

50 000 French in Champagne during February; 60 000 at St. Michiel; in May, 100 000 more at Arras and on Vimy Ridge.

He believed that the French, the British, and the Russians, with their reserves of manpower, were like gamblers holding a huge bankroll. Sooner or later their resources would prevail. They must attack and attack. Losses were immaterial provided the Germans were made to pay even a percentage of the Allied losses. German manpower would someday be exhausted.

Thus was born the horrible policy of attrition. Like Joffre, Sir John French too remained undaunted. He had ordered "deliberate and persistent" attacks by which the enemy would be "gradually and relentlessly worn down by exhaustion and loss until his defence collapses."

John Swettenham, *Canada and the First World War* (Toronto: Ryerson Press, 1969)

The Germans themselves were revolted by the senseless slaughter which resulted from the Allied orders. In September of 1915, there was a particularly bloody battle at Loos. Ten thousand Allied soldiers were ordered to advance across flat, open land against German machine guns. In just three and one-half hours, over 8000 were dead. The German losses were 2000. Historian Alan Clark comments:

One of the German battalion commanders spoke later of the revolting and nauseating impression made on them all as they watched the slaughter; so much so that after the retreat had begun they ceased fire. Before them was the *"Leichenfeld"* [field of corpses] of Loos, and, as among them

There are no finer or more gallant troops in the world [than the Canadians].

General Sir Horace Smith-Dorrien (a British general)

dozens of khaki-clad forms rose up once again and began to limp and crawl back to their own lines, "no shot was fired at them from the German trenches for the rest of the day, so great was the feeling of compassion and mercy for the enemy after such a victory."

Alan Clark, *The Donkeys* (New York: Universal Publishing, 1961)

The courage of Allied soldiers reached its peak in the battle of the Somme, in 1915. The morning of July 1 witnessed the worst disaster in British military history. In a few short hours, 57 000 men were killed, wounded, or missing. For the Newfoundland Regiment, which served as part of a British division, it was the worst day of the war. Of the 753 soldiers who went into action, all but 68 were either killed or wounded.

Vimy Ridge

The capture of Vimy Ridge on Easter Day, 1917, was the most significant achievement of the Canadian army in the First World War. For the first time in the war, Canadians of all four divisions had been united as one single fighting unit. British Columbians and Nova Scotians, French Canadians and Prairie farmers, together planned and courageously carried out an important breakthrough on the Western Front near the town of Vimy, France. The Canadians were by this time experienced and war-weathered soldiers. One veteran remembers:

We were an entirely different army from at the Somme, and I suppose that some of the terrible things that happened at the Somme were of some benefit in turning out the type of army that we had at Vimy. We had mastered our job. I think that's the basis of the whole show. Training, training, training! Master that gun! Master that gun!

The assault on Vimy Ridge remains the most famous of Canadian victories in war, but the cost in lives was very heavy. Of 60 000 Canadian casualties, there were 3598 who died in that battle. The victory was an entirely Canadian one, and it was accomplished with great courage and "esprit de corps." The accompanying photographs and recollections of veterans give us glimpses of this memorable battle.

Washing Up   *Public Archives Canada PA-1193*

A Canadian soldier tries to take his morning wash-up in a muddy shellhole early in 1917.

A Canadian Ambulance Driver on the Western Front in May, 1917   *Public Archives Canada PA-1305*

Public Archives Canada PA-1879

Vimy Ridge

Before the assault, the Ridge was pounded day and night for a full two weeks. From behind the Canadian lines, 983 guns at ninety-metre intervals fired three rounds per minute.

Vimy Ridge

As the Canadians advance, the machine gunners dig themselves into the shellholes.

Tanks provided some assistance to the Canadians as they moved toward the Ridge. Casualties during the attack were heavy.

Stretcher-bearers and German prisoners help bring back the wounded during the seige of Vimy Ridge.

After their determined and costly struggle, the Canadians are finally victorious. Here, at the crest of Vimy Ridge, Canadian soldiers view the battlefield.

The War in the Air

Many new technological developments were used for the first time in the Great War. However, these new inventions were seldom fully exploited. Like the tank, the aircraft was first used in battle on the Western Front. It came to be an essential weapon, not only in winning land battles but in protecting merchant shipping from submarines. It was even used for long-range strategic bombing, and this is how most airmen thought it would be used in the future.

In the Second World War, the air weapon would really come into its own. But even by the end of the First World War, nearly 25 000 Canadians had served with the Royal Naval Air Service, the Royal Flying Corps, and the Royal Air Force. This impressive contribution convinced many people that Canada should have an air force of its own. However, the government was reluctant to spend money for that purpose. Not until 1924 did the Royal Canadian Air Force come into being.

"Billy" Bishop

Public Archives Canada PA-1651

Among the greatest pilots of the Royal Flying Corps were several Canadians who won fame for their skill and courage in the air. Here Captain William A. Bishop stands in front of his aircraft, a Nieuport 17. "Billy" Bishop was Canada's most famous wartime pilot and was credited with 72 victories.

Why was the capture of Vimy Ridge such an important victory for Canada?

Why do you think new inventions, such as airplanes and the tank, were not used more effectively?

"War in the Air," by C. W. R. Nevinson   *National Gallery of Canada*

This is an artist's impression of the "dogfights" over the Western Front during the First World War.

The Bloodbath of Passchendaele

Another of the most senseless slaughters of Canadian soldiers occurred late in the war, near the crossroads village of Passchendaele in the Belgian flatlands of Flanders. After the shocking losses in the Somme offensive, it was hard for Canadians to believe that the same mistakes could be made again.

The region had been reclaimed from former swamps. Heavy October rains and damaged dikes had made this battlefield a stinking mass of mud and water. Tanks were useless, and the men sought shelter in slimy shellholes. Against the protests of Sir Arthur Currie, the Canadian commander, the British Commander-in-Chief Haig ordered the Canadian soldiers to take these few desolate hectares of mud.

Passchendaele

It was as if a powerful flood had swept over the entire landscape snapping off the trees and destroying everything in its path; and as if, in their recession, the waters had left tons of sludge and slimy pools where had been farms and fields. Everywhere was the jetsam of war: light locomotives, sunk to their boilers; guns, axle-deep in mud, pointing grotesquely at the sky; and sprawling bodies that neither side could clear because of the continuous shelling. The swollen flanks of dead horses and mules shone in the rain; human remains lay on every side. . . . A disgusting odour of sickly, sweet-smelling death pressed heavily on the senses.

John Swettenham, *Canada and the First world War* (Toronto: Ryerson Press, 1969)

In the end, the Canadians did the job asked of them. They pushed the Front 1.5 km into German territory. But at what cost! After two weeks of vicious fighting, 15 654 Canadians had lost their lives. What little value the victory had, if any at all, was lost in the spring of 1918, when the Germans regained this ground. Winston Churchill called the victory "a forlorn expenditure of valour and life without equal in futility."

Passchendaele remains today a symbol of the courageous sacrifice of the Canadian soldiers. It also stands out as a bitter comment on the arrogant insensitivity and gross stupidity of much of the military leadership of the First World War.

The Last 100 Days

At dawn on August 8, 1918, the Allied armies including the Canadian Corps launched a surprise offensive and punched a 13-km hole in the German lines at Amiens. For the next hundred days, Canadian troops helped to spearhead the final offensive of the war. The arrival of the American army had given the Allies the extra strength they needed.

The Germans, after four years of war, had suffered terrible losses. Although they continued to fight on bravely, the end was near. One after another, the French and then the Belgian towns fell to Canadian troops — Donai, Cambrai, Denain, Valenciennes, and finally Mons. It was in Mons, at eleven o'clock in the morning on November 11, 1918, that the war and the long struggle finally ended for the Canadians.

Armistice Day, November 11, 1918

The Great War ended on November 11, 1918. An unknown Canadian soldier describes his feelings:

Armistice Day dawned clear and crisp. No one was very happy. Now that we were out in the open and winning, it had to stop. "Berlin or Bust" now seemed ridiculous. The Armistice was officially announced in the Grande Place in Mons, Belgium, and the brigade bands played some airs. We had waited four years for this day, but no one laughed, no one cheered, no one got drunk!

The signing of the Armistice was the signal for many tremendous celebrations in the larger cities, particularly those farthest from the danger zone. But for the men under arms, it meant only that war-weary veterans would be under strict discipline and denied the campaign of movement to which we had looked forward. What to do? No war, no train for home, and so quiet one could hear one's hair growing. The thing was too sudden.

In Heather Robertson, A Terrible Beauty (Toronto: James Lorimer, 1977)

The Burial of Canadian Nurses Killed in a Bombing Raid in France, 1917   *Public Archives Canada PA-40264*

Homecoming

One fortunate Canadian son and brother returns home. About 60 000 did not.

My life is divided into three eras: before the war, during the war, and after the war.

Dan Vernon (Canadian veteran)

The First World War was over. More than 600 000 Canadians had served in the armed forces, and more than 60 000 had given their lives. The war had helped to unite the nation. Canadians who fought and served in the war did so with a common purpose. As one soldier put it:

I've always thought that the Canadian nation was, in fact, born on the battlefields of Europe. I'm sure that's true, that the fierce pride developed in the Canadians in their own identity, in their own nationhood, was a very real thing, and it survived over into the peace.

Canadians achieved a proud record on the battlefield and an incredible expansion of wealth and power at home. However, as we will see in the fourth chapter, Canada also underwent some social upheavals as a result of the war. In many ways, therefore, the influence of the First World War is still with us.

Summary

In August, 1914, war came to Europe, which had not known a major war for a full century. Many Europeans looked upon the war as a brief, even exciting, adventure. In Canada, people gave little thought to the events in Europe until Great Britain's declaration of war on Germany in 1914. This brought Canada and the rest of the British Empire into the war as well.

Four years later, more than 30 million were dead, including 60 000 young Canadians, in the worst conflict in human history. By 1918, European civilization was largely in ruins, and some of the old empires had vanished. A war which had begun with flamboyant uniforms and enthusiastic fanfare ended with airplanes, tanks and trenches, gas attacks, and undreamed-of loss of life.

Canada had entered the war as a loyal British colony. It came out a united nation, proud of its contribution and its achievements and ready to play a larger role in international affairs. Canada was also sombered by the awful cost in lives and by social upheavals which the war caused at home. In the fourth chapter, we will examine the effects of the First World War on our home front.

CHAPTER THREE

Canada in the Second World War

When the surviving soldiers of the Great War returned to their homes and their families, the world they had known was drastically changed. In four years, nearly twenty million people had died as a direct result of the conflict. European economies had been shattered. A large part of a generation of their young men had disappeared. Europeans sought to pick up the pieces and start rebuilding. In the twenty years following the armistice, there were great economic, social, and political upheavals. These upheavals would bring the world into war once again. The twenty years between the wars might be seen as really only a break in what was one great war. It began in 1914 and was to end in 1945.

Origins of the Second World War

Many historians say that the seeds of the Second World War were sown in the peace settlement which concluded the First World War. In 1919, the Treaty of Versailles was drawn up by the victorious Allies after six months of negotiation. Canada, having earned its right on the bloodied battlefields of France and Belgium, participated in the discussions as part of the British delegation.

The Versailles Treaty changed many of the borders of Europe, regrouping it according to nationalities. Provinces in the Empire, such as Czechoslovakia and Yugoslavia, now became nations. Austria and Hungary became separate nations. Germany lost a great deal of territory. Alsace-Lorraine went to France, and a large part of Germany's eastern territory went to the newly formed state of Poland.

"Infantry near Nijmegen, Holland," by Alex Colville

Canadian infantry return after an exhausting tour of duty in the flooded lands between the Waal and the Neder Rijn during the winter of 1944-45.

The peace treaty was extremely hard on Germany, because the victorious nations wanted revenge. They unfairly blamed Germany for starting the war. Germany was forced to shoulder responsibility for all the destruction of the war. The fact that Germany had wanted only to reduce tensions between the Austrians and Serbs in 1914 was totally ignored. The aggressive actions of other nations in starting the war were also ignored.

On June 28, 1919, the Versailles Treaty was handed to the leader of the German delegation, Count Brockdorff-Rantzau. He was enraged at the harsh terms dictated to his government, but he had no other choice than to sign it. In doing so, he said:

The peace to be concluded with Germany was to be a peace of right, not a peace of might. . . .
   The peace document shows that none of [the] repeated solemn assurances has been kept.
   To begin with the territorial questions:
   In the West, a purely German territory on the Saar with a population of at least 650 000 inhabitants is to be separated from the German Empire for at least fifteen years merely for the reason that claims are asserted to the coal abounding there. . . .

Although President Wilson of the United States, in his speech of October 20th, 1916, has acknowledged that "no single fact caused the war, but that in the last analysis the whole European system is in a deeper sense responsible for the war, with its combination of alliances and understandings, a complicated texture of intrigues and espionage that unfailingly caught the whole family of nations in its meshes," "that the present war is not so simply to be explained, and that its roots reach deep into the dark soil of history," Germany is to acknowledge that Germany and her allies are responsible for all damages. . . . Apart from the consideration that there is no incontestable legal foundation for the obligation for reparation imposed upon Germany, the amount of such compensation is to be determined by a commission nominated solely by Germany's enemies.

Harsh Terms for Germany in the Treaty of Versailles

Article 42. Germany is forbidden to maintain or construct any fortifications either on the left bank of the Rhine or on the right bank to the west of a line drawn 50 kilometres to the east. . . .
Article 45. As compensation for the destruction of the coal mines in the north of France and as part payment towards the total reparation due . . . Germany cedes to France . . . the coal mines situated in the Saar Basin. . . .
Article 119. Germany renounces . . . all her rights and titles over her overseas possessions. . . .
Article 159. The German military forces shall be demobilized and reduced as prescribed hereinafter.
Article 160. By a date which must not be later than March 31, 1920, the German Army must not comprise more than seven divisions of infantry and three divisions of cavalry.
   After that date the . . . Army of . . . Germany must not exceed one hundred thousand men, including officers. . . .
   The total officers . . . must not exceed four thousand. . . .
Artilce 198. The armed forces of Germany must not include any military or naval air forces. . . .
Article 231. The Allied and Associated Governments affirm and Germany accepts the responsibility of Germany and her allies for causing all the loss and damage to which the Allied and Associated Governments and their nationals have been subjected as a consequence of the war. . . .
Article 232. The Allied and Associated Governments recognize that the resources of Germany are not adequate . . . to make complete reparation for all such loss and damage.
   The Allied and Associated Governments, however, require, and Germany undertakes, that she will make compensation for all damage done to the civilian population of the Allied and Associated Powers and to their property during the . . . belligerency. . . .
Article 233. The amount of the above damage for which compensation is to be made by Germany shall be determined by an Inter-Allied Commission. . . .
Article 428. As a guarantee for the execution of the present Treaty by Germany, the German territory situated to the west of the Rhine . . . will be occupied by Allied and Associated troops for a period of fifteen years. . . .
Article 431. If before the expiration of the period of fifteen years Germany complies with all the undertakings resulting from the present Treaty, the occupying forces will be withdrawn.

*What were the causes of another world war just twenty years after
the First World War?*

*Do you think the Treaty of Versailles was fair to Germany? How
might it have been improved?*

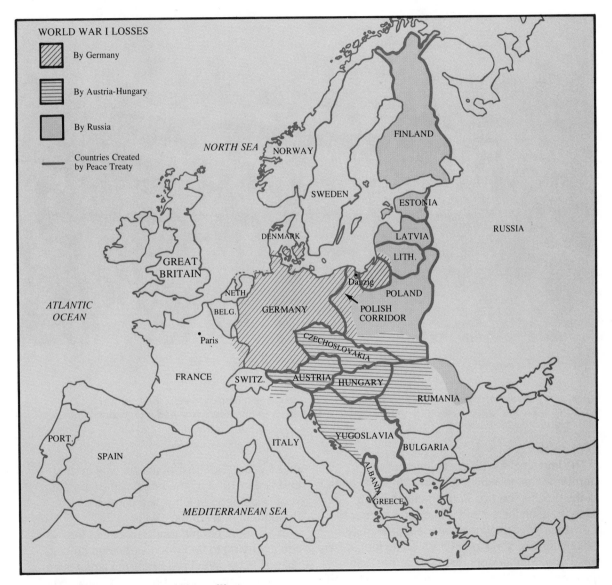

Europe after the Treaty of Versailles

Post-War Discontent

Canada had some major disturbances as returning soldiers found little employment in the post-war depression. Among the worst was the general strike in Winnipeg. Events there reached a climax on June 21, 1919. Here, crowds attempt to tip over a trolley car.

The impact of the peace settlement on Germany was devastating. Being forced to bear all the guilt for the war was a heavy burden. The huge drain on the country's economy to meet the "reparation" payments made it extremely difficult for Germany to get back on its feet at the war's end. Furthermore, the new democratic government of Germany, which had been forced to sign the Versailles Treaty, was blamed by embittered returning soldiers for having "sold out" to the Allies.

Still, the 1920s were a time of recovery, a time of trying to forget the war years and build for the future. People were becoming optimistic during these years. But their optimism was quickly crushed in 1929 by the beginning of a great worldwide depression which continued throughout most of the 1930s.

In Canada, people travelled across the country trying to find work. Repeated crop failures in the West made difficult times even worse. In Canada and throughout the world, frustrated and hungry people struck out bitterly against the governments which seemed responsible for such hardships. But the governments appeared to be helpless. The world had become too interdependent for one nation to solve all its economic problems alone.

Humanitarianism is the expression of stupidity and cowardice.

Adolf Hitler, 1935

The Canadian government set up Relief Camps for unemployed single males. Operated by the Department of National Defence, they were located in isolated places and were under military control. In the mid-1930s, many Canadians began protesting against conditions in the Relief Camps. On June 19, 1938, some western Relief Camp workers staged a sit-down strike in a post office. The RCMP and Vancouver police violently cleared out the building. This incident, known as "Bloody Sunday," effectively ended the workers' protests against their conditions and wages of twenty cents a day.

The Rise of Fascism

The Great Depression hit Europe even harder than it hit Canada. In Germany alone, six million people were unemployed in 1932. Desperate men and women, looking for a way out, began to put the blame on innocent "scapegoats." Dictatorial leaders arose, who promised stability and jobs. They attracted a large number of supporters. In Italy, Germany, and Spain, democratic governments gave way to Benito Mussolini, Adolf Hitler, and General Francisco Franco. In the 1930s, there was hardly a European country without its fascist party of some kind.

In Germany, this fascism was called "Nazism." It was based on an extreme nationalistic pride. It offered a vision of a national leader who would "save" the country from its troubles and rid it of its supposed enemies. Fascism called for a total dictatorship, a "totalitarian" form of government. This was supported by a strong army and highly trained secret police. The personal freedom of individual citizens was lost.

Germany still felt wronged by the Versailles Treaty and was still angry. It was in a mood to find scapegoats to punish for its suffering. The democratic government established after the First World War had never taken a firm hold because it had too many difficulties to face. The Nazi leader, Adolf Hitler, made it one of the scapegoats, saying it was responsible for all Germany's troubles.

He also claimed that Germans belonged to the supposedly superior Aryan race; and he decided to punish and even destroy other, so-called "inferior," races. Among these, he saw as his chief enemy the Jewish people, whom he

A Hitler Youth Rally *Public Archives Canada C-24954*

wrongly blamed for Germany's troubles.

When Hitler came to power in 1933, he reduced the unemployment and replaced the feeble democratic government with a highly organized political machine. With an aggressive foreign policy, he won back many of the areas Germany had lost in the Versailles Treaty. His extreme nationalism restored the self-confidence of many Germans and won him much support. But the price the Germans would have to pay for this national self-esteem and the economic benefits soon became all too apparent.

All German citizens lost many human rights. Some lost all their personal freedom. Political opposition was not tolerated. There was a shocking conquest of "non-Aryan" peoples. Before the end of the Second World War, fifteen to twenty million people had been executed by the Nazis. Six million of them were systematically murdered simply because they were Jewish.

During the 1930s, international relations were becoming generally chaotic. The League of Nations, a forerunner of the United Nations, had been formed after the First World War to maintain world peace. However, it was never very successful.

Mussolini's armies invaded the ancient African state of Abyssinia (Ethiopia) in 1935, pitting bombers against spears. The League was outraged, but it refused to take effective action. The strongest stand taken at the League of Nations meeting in Geneva, Switzerland, was the one taken by the Canadian representative, Dr. W. A. Riddell. He believed that the League members could stop Italian aggression if they would impose a complete trade embargo on Italy — especially on her imports of oil, petroleum, coal, iron, and steel. In November, 1935, Dr. Riddell moved that such an embargo be imposed.

Prime Minister Mackenzie King was alarmed because it might seem that Canada was taking a leadership role in this matter. He therefore refused to back Dr. Riddell. So an important opportunity for Canada to lead the way in standing up to an act of aggression was missed.

The remembered horrors of the First World War, and the influence of public opinion, led the Allied countries to agree to even the most humiliating terms with Hitler as long as they could stop short of war. Appeasement only fed the Nazi dictator's appetite all the more. With Japan waging a war of expansion in the Far East and Italy following Germany's example, the aggressors — especially Hitler — became bolder and stronger with each new move that went unchallenged by the rest of the world.

While Mussolini was carving out his new "Roman Empire" in Africa, General Franco's fascists were consolidating their power in Spain after winning a viciously fought civil war. About 1250 Canadians volunteered to fight against Franco, although they had no support from the Canadian government. They called themselves the Mackenzie-Papineau Battalion. Their motto was, "1837-1937: Fascism shall be destroyed."

By the late 1930s, the democratic nations realized that they might soon have to take a stand. Hitler was rapidly expanding his power. Taking advantage of the refusal of Britain, France, and the United States to stop him, he stepped up his aggression. He first reoccupied the Rhineland, which had been forbidden by the Versailles Treaty. This was followed, in March of 1938, by the invasion of Austria and its annexation, or *"Anschluss,"* into the Third Reich. A year later, Hitler took over Czechoslovakia.

In the summer of 1939, Hitler made impossible demands on Poland, whose independence had been guaranteed by both Britain and France. In the evening of August 31, 1939, the German army crossed the Polish border. The Second World War had begun.

Why might Hitler have had the support of the German people?

How can we account for the refusal of democratic nations to stand up to Hitler, Mussolini, and Franco in the 1930s? Do you think it was justified?

The Deportations

Yivo Institute for Jewish Research

With the outbreak of the War, Nazi policy shifted from persecution to internment of Jews in concentration camps. Throughout occupied Europe, Jews were forced into ghettos which served as way stations for "The Final Solution."

Here, terrified women and children are being rounded up for deportation during the Warsaw Ghetto uprising in April, 1943. This photograph was described by an eyewitness: "People run from all staircases" at the signal that their street has been sealed off. "Nervously, on the run, they clothe themselves in whatever is handy. Some descend as they are, sometimes straight from bed; others are carrying everything they can possibly take along. . . . Trembling, they form groups in front of the house. They are not allowed to talk, but they still try to gain the policeman's pity. From nearby houses similar groups of trembling, completely desperate people arrive and form into one long column. . . . Two, three shots signify the death of those who did not heed the call and remained in their homes."

The Holocaust

European Jews had for centuries been targets of popular prejudice and superstition. They were often used as scapegoats by their governments. Anti-semitism was a cornerstone of Nazi policy, and Hitler's rise to power in 1933 marked the start of vicious anti-Jewish persecution. German Jews lost their vote and were prevented from holding jobs in the civil service, schools, and universities. Their businesses were boycotted; their writers couldn't publish; and they were forbidden to marry people of another religion. Jewish children were expelled from public schools.

In November, 1938, thousands of Jewish synagogues, hospitals, and orphanages were burned to the ground, and many Jews were sent to concentration camps. Hundreds of thousands attempted to escape Nazi Germany. Some, like Albert Einstein and Sigmund Freud, succeeded; but most did not.

Like the Vietnamese "boat people" in 1979, these people faced almost certain death. In 1939, however, the world's democracies did very little to help. Of the one million Jews seeking refuge, Canada admitted a mere 4000. Although personally convinced that the Jewish people of Europe faced certain extinction, Immigration Commissioner Frederick Blair kept Canada's doors closed to most refugees. Many concerned Canadians tried to persuade the Canadian government to act, but Prime Minister King continued to resist all their appeals.

When the war began, European borders were sealed. Hope of saving the refugees was lost. In July of 1941, Hitler approved plans for the organized murder of all Jewish citizens in Germany and in the countries under Nazi occupation. Huge death camps — such as those at Auschwitz, Treblinka, and Dachau — systematically used poison gas and crematoria to destroy millions of human lives. At Auschwitz alone, between 1 750 000 and 2 500 000 men, women, and children were killed.

Not only Jews suffered. Millions of others, including German political prisoners, Soviet and Polish civilians, prisoners of war, and European Gypsies were also methodically murdered. Genocide on this scale has only happened once in modern history. That it could have happened in a country as highly civilized as Germany shows us that, given a particular set of circumstances, it could happen anywhere. The gas chambers and ovens of Nazi death camps stand as a terrible reminder of what can follow when discrimination against minorities is taken to its extreme conclusion.

Declarations of War

After learning of the invasion of Poland on the night of August 31, 1939, Canadians waited for Britain's response. It came on Sunday morning, September 3. Neville Chamberlain, the British Prime Minister, announced his country's declaration of war against Germany.

In 1914, Canada had been automatically at war when Britain went to war. But by 1939, Canada had gained the right to make its own decisions. This was brought about by the Statute of Westminster in 1931. At the Imperial Conference of 1926, British delegates under Lord Balfour had replaced the term "British Empire" with the expression "Commonwealth." The so-called Balfour Declaration described Great Britain and the dominions as:

. . . autonomous communities within the British Empire, equal in status, in no way subordinate one to another in any aspect of their external affairs, though united by a common allegiance to the Crown, and freely associated as members of the British Commonwealth of Nations.

When the British Parliament passed the Statute of Westminster, it gave Canada and the other dominions the constitutional right to make their own decisions in all affairs. After Britain declared war on Germany in 1939, therefore, Canadian Prime Minister King insisted that the Canadian Parliament be recalled. In the House of Commons on September 8, he argued for an independent Canadian declaration of war.

Parliament almost unanimously agreed. On the following Sunday morning, September 10, Canada was at war.

The Canadian War Effort

At first, the Canadian contribution to the war was to be largely in the form of providing war materials. There was no immediate decision to raise a large army for overseas service. The Canadian government developed a seven-part plan which set up the following goals:

1. The defence and security of Canada
2. Vital food supplies for Britain
3. A massive industrial program for weapons and ammunition
4. Training courses for Allied pilots
5. Development of the Royal Canadian Air Force (RCAF) for home defence and overseas service
6. Development of the Royal Canadian Navy for home defence and convoy escort duty
7. Development of a sizeable army for home defence and overseas duty

One of the earliest proposals to be implemented was the British Commonwealth Air Training Plan, in December of 1939. It involved the construction of 64 schools in Canada. These schools would train 20 000 pilots a year from all participating Commonwealth countries.

Under the guidance of C. D. Howe, Minister of Munitions and Supply, Canadian industry expanded rapidly to produce weapons, explosives, aircraft, and ships. This brought about full employment and unparalleled prosperity by 1943, and it laid the basis of Canada's post-war industrial boom. Canadian farmers also increased food production to meet the wartime needs.

As in the First World War, Canada quickly mobilized an untrained division for overseas duty. By December of 1939, the First Canadian Division, consisting of about 23 000 troops, landed in Britain. A second division was soon to follow.

Between September of 1939 and May of 1940, there was comparatively little action. The Germans had quickly overrun Poland. But on the Western Front, the Germans and the Allied armies occupied fixed positions and engaged in little fighting.

Then came the sudden German invasions of Norway in April of 1940, and of the Netherlands and Belgium in May of that year. In Norway, the Allies waged a losing battle against the invaders; in Belgium, there was a quick surrender. This allowed the German divisions to move into France, driving the British back to the English Channel.

From Dunkirk, the entire British Expeditionary Force and a sizeable portion of the French army were evacuated to England in one of the greatest rescue operations in history. Unfortunately, all the heavy equipment had to be left behind. By June of 1940, France had collapsed. Hitler was left with no opposition on the Continent. For a long while, a Nazi invasion of Britain was widely predicted.

Although the invasion never came, Britain stood alone in Europe in 1940 and 1941. During the fall of 1940, the German air force conducted continuous bombing raids on British cities and caused terrible damage.

When Italy entered the war on the German side in June of 1940, British forces soon became occupied in the Mediterranean and North Africa. Initially, they were successful against the Italian navy and army. But they were driven back in North Africa by the Germans, who came to Italy's aid.

In 1941, the war began to take on truly worldwide dimensions. In June, Hitler decided to attack Russia. On December 7, the Japanese attacked the United States at Pearl Harbor, Hawaii. This immediately brought the United States into the conflict. Canada and Great Britain also declared war on Japan. Canadian soldiers who had been stationed in Hong Kong suffered heavy losses when their garrison was overwhelmed on Christmas Day in 1941.

Throughout 1942, the Allies built up a large force in Britain to prepare for a future invasion of Europe. The Canadians participated in these preparations. In January, 1942, Canada's overseas forces consisted of five divisions and two brigades. They comprised the First Canadian Army, the largest military formation in Canada's history.

Canada's Air Force and Navy

Although the army was still under training in Britain, the Canadian air force and navy had been actively participating in the war since 1939. The Royal Canadian Air Force grew at an incredible rate and played a major role in the war against Germany. It increased from less than 4000 in 1939 to 206 000 by the end of 1943.

During the war, Canada had a bomber wing in North Africa, a fighter wing in northwestern Europe, and its Bomber Command in the strategic air offensive against Germany. In addition, there were tens of thousands of Canadians in other Canadian squadrons which were attached to the RAF; thousands of them were in southeast Asia. Our casualty rates in the Bomber Command were much higher than those in the army or navy. The significance of the RCAF in the Second World War was tremendous.

During the same period, the Royal Canadian Navy increased its number of ships and personnel. As the war continued, the Navy played an increasingly important role in all parts of the world. It carried on coastal operations in Northwest Europe, in the Mediterranean, and in the Pacific Ocean.

By far the biggest maritime role that Canada played was in the Battle of the Atlantic. This battle kept open the lifeline to Britain. If it had been lost, the war might have had a different outcome. If Canada had not generously contributed men, aircraft, and ships to the battle, and if the ports of Canada and Newfoundland had not been available, the war would certainly have dragged on much longer.

As it was, most of Canada's 375 fighting ships and a large proportion of the 23 000 men and women of the Royal Canadian Navy were directly involved in the safe passage of convoys to and from Europe. Ten squadrons of the RCAF based in Canada and Newfoundland and six attached to the British Coastal Command also played a leading part in this vital task. It resulted in the defeat of the German U-boats which were attacking Allied shipping.

"Zero Hour," by William Dring

*Canadian War Museum, National Museum of Man,
National Museums of Canada Acc. 7809*

Canadian pilots are about to take off for a bombing mission over Germany. The voices in the briefing room are low and calm, but artist William Dring has caught the real tension felt by each person present.

Protecting the Lifeline

Public Archives Canada 0-93-1

This long-range maritime patrol aircraft of the Royal Canadian Air Force assists the ships of the Royal Canadian Navy in helping to escort one of the great Atlantic convoys from Halifax to Great Britain in 1944. Without this protection, enemy submarines would soon have destroyed this critical lifeline of war supplies from North America.

The Dieppe Raid, 1942

In 1942, the Russians were being pressed hard by the Germans. Russia insisted that the Allies open a second front. The Allies were not ready for such an invasion. But they decided to test the German defences by attempting a raid on the French seaport town of Dieppe.

On August 19, 1942, a force of 5000 troops from the Canadian Second Division and 1000 British commandos, together with some American troops, launched the raid on Dieppe. There was devastating German fire. The attacking forces established themselves on the shore, but they failed to make any major breach in the German defences. The Canadians suffered 3367 casualties, the Germans 333. It was said that what the Allies learned from the Dieppe raid ensured the success of the Normandy invasion in 1944. But controversy over the strategic value of this raid still continues.

Ross Munro, a Canadian war correspondent, witnessed the tragic scene on the beach at Puys after the Royal Regiment had landed:

> When I got to Puys, it was just a carnage. I never saw anything like it in the remaining years of the war, following the Canadians on all their campaigns. This was the worst battle I have ever seen. It was my first one, so it sticks in my memory very vividly to this day. It was at that time when I could see the Puys thing was gone, because the whole slope was just littered with khaki bodies of wounded and killed Royals. It was unbelievable to see that gulch just covered with Canadians. And they were lying around the beach, and the tremendous fire from the buildings and from the top of the gulch. You could see that things were in a desperate shape then, and very few people actually got up the gulch. It was a very small party that actually got there.

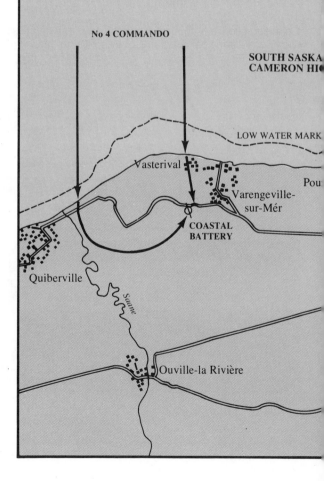

Landings and movements ashore by Canadian units a shown by solid white arrows.

Movements by flanking British units are shown by solid black arrows.

Movements planned but not completed are shown by broken black arrows.

No 4 COMMANDO

SOUTH SASKA
CAMERON HI

LOW WATER MARK

Vasterival

Pou

Varengeville-
sur-Mér

COASTAL
BATTERY

Quiberville

Saane

Ouville-la Rivière

> *It is not enough to shudder over bloated bodies floating up on the beach, or of maggotted corpses piled up like cordwood. All the poetic fervour in the world against war will not abolish it if we do not understand how wars begin and how peace can be made.*

Norman Cousins, *Saturday Review.*

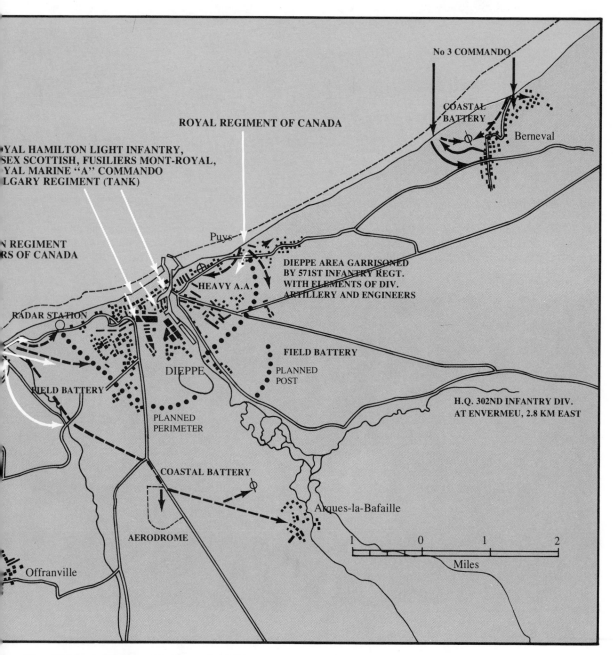

The Raid on Dieppe 19 August 1942

The Dieppe Raid

Public Archives Canada C-14160

Two of the 907 Canadians who lost their lives on the beaches of Dieppe, France, in a disastrous raid on the morning of August 19, 1942. The Canadians fought bravely against incredible odds; but of the 4963 men who left England that morning, 3367 of them were killed, wounded, or taken prisoner by two o'clock in the afternoon.

Canadian Prisoners

Public Archives Canada C-29588

Many of the survivors of the tragic Dieppe Raid are taken prisoners by the Germans and marched through the streets of Dieppe.

The Italian Campaign

The First Canadian Division landed with the Allies in Sicily on July 9, 1943. After overrunning Sicily, the Canadians and the British together crossed the Straits of Messina to the Italian mainland, reaching it on September 3, 1943. Matthew Halton, a Canadian war correspondent, describes the landing:

> We are in Italy. The First Canadian Division, with brother formations of the United States Eighth Army, is in Italy, unopposed. We made an assault, landing at dawn today, and made the first breach in the walls of Nazi Europe; and it cost us not one single man. As I speak, a few German shells are landing on our positions; but at dawn today, when we crashed the gates of Europe, not one machine-gun bullet broke the silence, not one enemy shell fell among our landing craft, not one mine exploded in our faces.

The Advance in Sicily   *Public Archives Canada PA-21804*

This patrol of the First Infantry Division near Ispica commandeered donkey carts to haul heavy weapons and equipment.

The Normandy Invasion

On June 6, 1944 ("D-Day"), the Third Canadian Division crossed the Channel with Allied troops and at last established the second front in Normandy, France. The Second Corps, under General Guy Simonds, engaged in the desperate fighting which closed the Falaise Gap in August of 1944. In the autumn of that year, the Canadian Army under General Crerar cleared the Channel ports and later opened the Scheldt estuary.

The First Canadian Corps left Italy in March of 1945 to join the rest of the Canadian Army, which was fighting with other Allied forces. They cleared the Rhineland and liberated the Netherlands. The Germans surrendered on May 7.

The collapse of Japan, in August of 1945, removed the possibility of further Canadian involvement in the war. World War II was over.

Embarkation

Public Archives Canada C-24717

For the second time in twenty-five years, young Canadians left to fight a war in Europe. Here General McNaughton's First Overseas Division embarks on December 18, 1939.

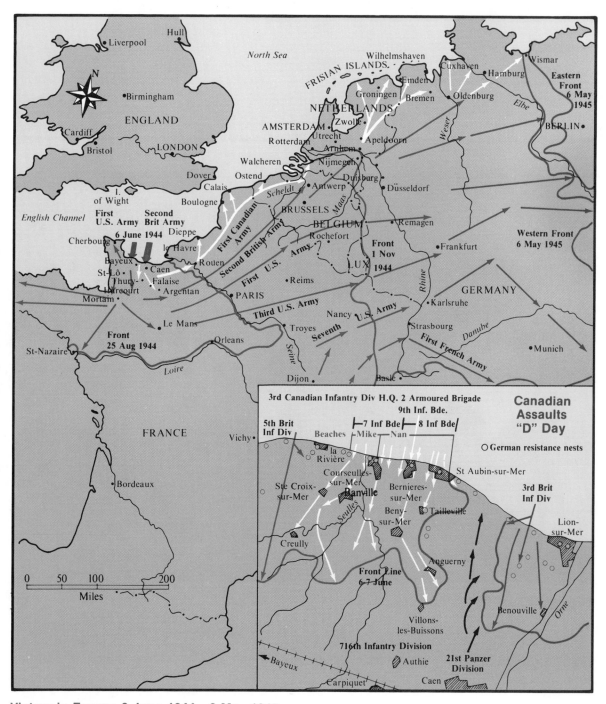

Victory in Europe 6 June 1944 - 8 May 1945

Victory at Last!

Happy members of the Canadian armed forces celebrate the end of the Second World War.

Summary

Many historians have seen the Second World War as really a continuation of a war that began in 1914 with a 20-year intermission from 1919 to 1939. Hitler played the greatest role in bringing about the Second World War. It can be argued that if the terms of the Versailles peace treaty had not been so harsh, the political turmoil and economic collapse which plagued Germany after the First World War would never had occurred, and Hitler might never have gained so much popular support in that country. When Hitler began to close his grip on Germany in the 1930s and Mussolini and Franco consolidated their dictatorships in Italy and Spain, the rest of world stood by and watched until it was too late. Events in Europe and the Far East worsened, and the Second World War began in 1939.

Canada independently declared war on Germany a week after the British had done so. Once in the war, Canadians fought with skill, determination, and great sacrifice as they had in the First World War. When it ended in 1945, Canada had become a widely respected nation with an outstanding military record.

CHAPTER FOUR

Canada on the Home Front

In the thirty years between 1914 and 1945, Canada was an important participant in each of the world wars. Except for one week at the beginning of the Second World War, Canada was at war from start to finish — almost ten full years, one decade out of three. No country could have survived such an ordeal unchanged. Canada certainly changed from an agricultural and rural population to a modern industrial society. In addition, war caused upheavals in political and social life.

Economic Growth

The First World War had a profound impact on Canada. In 1914, Canada was still mainly an agricultural country. A majority of its people lived on farms and in small villages and towns. The beginnings of an industrial economy were already in evidence. However, the growth of industry was slow. Manufacturers were still trying to increase their efficiency in order to become competitive abroad.

The start of the First World War greatly changed this scene. The products of Canadian industry and agriculture were immediately much in demand by the Allies. Canadians, volunteering by the tens of thousands to serve overseas, created labour shortages in factories and on farms. Industry increased its efficiency by standardizing parts and breaking each job into simple repetitive tasks. Agricultural production was improved by the manufacture and use of new farm machinery.

Most Canadians were motivated by a strong sense of patriotic duty to give their utmost effort to wartime production. But in all wars, there are individuals whose major consideration is personal profit. War is an extremely profitable business for many industries. Canada's purchase of many thousands of Ross rifles, for

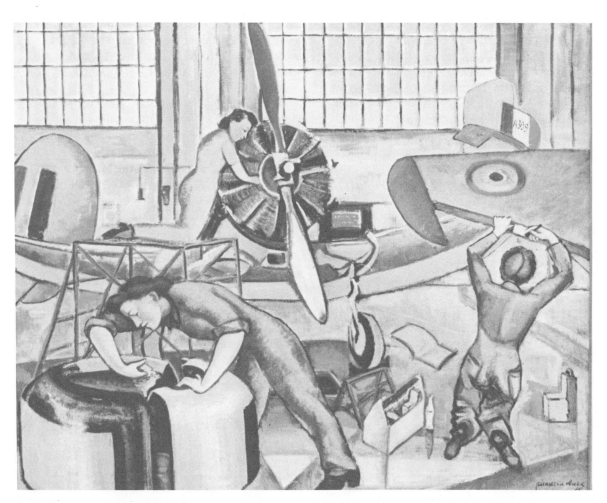

**"Maintenance Jobs in the Hangar,"
by Paraskeva Clark**

Canadian War Museum, National Museum of Man, National Museums of Canada Acc. 14085

instance, made the munitions company rich; but it was responsible for the deaths of Canadian soldiers. The Ross jammed repeatedly during rapid fire, while the defenceless soldier "tore at the rifle bolts with bleeding hands, sobbing with exasperation." More than once, the rifle killed a soldier who was trying to shoot with it.

Many Canadians began, in the First World War, to speak of "war profiteering," and of the government's stupidity in spending money on such worthless things as the Ross rifles. The Canadian public also complained loudly of the high prices for essential consumer goods. Even when peace came, there were no effective controls on prices. This created hardships for returning soldiers as well as for people on fixed incomes.

In the Second World War, there were early government regulations to prevent excessive war profiteering. By fixing prices and freezing wages, the Wartime Prices and Trade Board avoided wartime inflation. Consequently, the standard of living for most Canadians became higher than ever before in the nation's history.

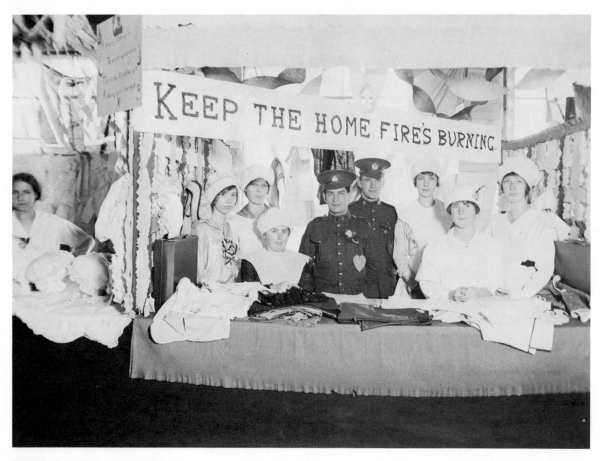

Red Cross Volunteers, 1917

City of Toronto Archives, James Collection

**War may come and war may go,
But we'll go on forever — if we can.**

The Montreal Daily Star, 1918

How War Affected Canadian Women

The First World War is often seen as a dramatic watershed in the growing acceptance of women as equal partners in Canadian society. In both wars, women played an important part in the Canadian economy. Departing men caused serious labour shortages. These were soon filled by women.

In the First World War, as many as 20 000 were employed in making shells and aircraft. Thousands more worked the farms. Women also went to work in the civil service, and in banking and insurance firms. Well over 10 000 entered business life for the first time.

There were, of course, also thousands of women serving overseas, mostly as nurses. Many of them were on the front lines. Some earned decorations for valour. A good number never returned.

When the First World War started, Canadian women had not yet won the right to vote. The war made a great change in their status as they took over more and more responsibilities at home and overseas. By the end of the war, the Canadian government had passed the Wartime Elections Act, which was the beginning of full and equal franchise for Canadian women.

In the Second World War, there were nearly 50 000 women in uniform. Women in the work force rose from 638 000 in 1939 to over a million in 1943. This was more than all the armed forces put together.

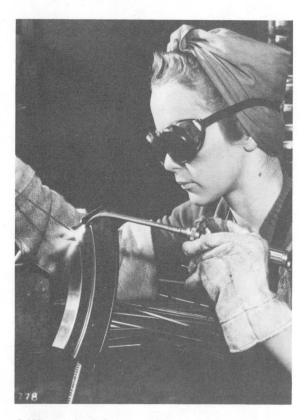

A Woman's Job

Public Archives Canada C-75211

Ethel Mitchell, a welder, works on a gun
magazine in a Second World War munitions
factory. By the end of the war, women had
welded 6500 tanks and assembled 244 000
machine guns.

Ship-Building

Public Archives Canada C-81420

Thousands of Canadian women, like this
ship-builder, were employed in heavy industry
during the Second World War. She is riveting
steel hulls in a Pictou, Nova Scotia, shipyard.

Would propaganda techniques be as effective today as they were during the First and Second World Wars? Explain why?

Does the home front know what is really going on at the battle front during a war?

Recruitment

As initial enthusiasm for the First World War began to fade, the Canadian government looked for ways to maintain voluntary enlistments in the army. Recruitment drives became a top priority.

News of the rising slaughter in Europe and the incompetence of the military leadership was censored. Up and down the country, fiery speeches appealing to patriotism and loyalty were made by political and religious leaders. Newspapers were loud in their support of the war. Posters were used in both wars to get people to enlist. Posters and newspapers were especially influential in the First World War, because this was a time without radio or television.

As support for the war rose, young men who appeared old enough to be in the army were branded as cowards or slackers if they stayed home. Women approached them in the streets of Vancouver, Toronto, and Montreal and pinned on their lapels white feathers symbolizing cowardice.

In them days, it was rather annoying to go out at all because the men in uniform, when you would walk down the street, they'd come and tap you on the shoulder and say "Why ain't you in the army?" And I used to have difficulty even when I told them I had bad ears because I'd had scarlet fever. "Go on, try again. Try again." — *Martin Colby*

In Toronto at that time there was a Captain Lawson. Saturday night was his big night for recruiting. As a senior recruiting officer, he used to hold up a Union Jack and offer to give any man that would enlist a piece of that Union Jack to take with him to Europe to show what he was fighting for. And, as I recall, there was many a man awakened up a Saturday morning or Sunday morning after having been indulging in alcoholic spirits the night before . . . much to his surprise, he awakened to find he had become enlisted in His Majesty's Services!

As the war progressed, one of my brother's chums, Harry Bowl, he joined the infantry at the age of sixteen and went overseas almost at once. And he returned the following year, having lost his right leg in France. I can recall that, at that time, anyone that didn't join up was referred to as a slacker or a coward. I can recall that Harry Bowl had an artificial leg.

The ladies of Toronto should have been doing something else, that is, they should have been involved in war munitions work. They were going around with turkey feather dusters which they loaded with talcum powder, and they used to shower the powder over any person that they thought was a slacker. And my brother's chum, who had already lost one leg at the age of sixteen, he received the same treatment, and so he was covered with flour down near the City Hall. He drew his trousers up to show his artificial leg, and he gave the ladies quite a scolding because he told them he thought they should be doing something more useful. — *George Wilkes*

Daphne Read, Ed., The Great War and Canadian Society (Toronto: New Hogtown Press, 1978)

A Common Type of Poster during the First World War

City of Toronto Archives, James Collection

One Technique Used to Encourage Enlistment

City of Toronto Archives, James Collection

Maintaining the War Effort

In addition to their all-out efforts in industrial output and in many volunteer organizations, Canadians were asked to conserve food and to invest money in the wars.

Food was desperately needed by the Allied armies. In the First World War, the government asked Canadians not to hoard food. In the Second World War, it established the Wartime Prices and Trade Board to control the economy of Canada. The Board had power to control the price, supply, and distribution of all goods and services. In 1941, the Board froze prices and wages. In 1942, it set up a food rationing program for essential food products. Families were issued ration books, which allowed them just certain amounts of flour, sugar, tea, coffee, and other commodities a month.

Large funds were needed for the high costs of war. The government raised these funds by selling "Victory Bonds" to the Canadian public. Income taxes were also introduced in the country at this time.

Conscription in World War I

As the First World War dragged on, the support of Canadians began to lessen. Stories of the incredible loss of human life on the Western Front began to filter in despite official censorship. Each day, newspapers were filled with column after column of the names of Canadians who were dead, wounded, or missing. It is not surprising that people became less willing to enlist.

Canadian War Museum, National Museum of Man, National Museums of Canada

Raising War Funds

This poster was widely used in the First World War to encourage Canadians to make a personal loan to the government.

Do you think that rationing might ever be used in peacetime? Why?

Should a government have the right to force some of its citizens to fight for the country? Why or why not?

In the summer of 1917, the government passed the Military Service Bill, which called for conscription for overseas service. Sir Wilfrid Laurier, a former prime minister, refused to believe that conscription was necessary. In a debate in Parliament, he called for a referendum to allow Canadians to express their views.

> The law of the land . . . emphatically declares that no man in Canada shall be subjected to compulsory military service except to repel invasion or for the defence of Canada. . . . It is the people who must change the law . . . and not this Parliament, which I claim has not the right. . . . What I propose is that we should have a referendum and a consultation of the people upon this question. . . . Is that an unfair situation? Is that an unfair appeal?

Prime Minister Robert Borden refused to do this. He said there was only one honourable choice for Canada:

> We are all proud that Canada has played a splendid and notable part in this war. Is Canada content to relax her efforts in the most critical period of a war which concerns her heritage, her status and her liberty? . . . The men at the front have answered the call, they have given glorious service, they have put aside all material considerations; duty alone has been their ideal. . . . I know from my personal experience that they cannot realize the thought that their country, which so summoned them to her service, will be content to desert and humiliate them.

Bordon stated emphatically:

> There are only two alternatives — to let our forces dwindle from four divisions to three, from three to two, and perhaps from two to one, or to bring aid by other means than an appeal for voluntary service. This is the problem which confronts Canada today.

In an emotional reply, Sir Wilfrid Laurier warned that conscription would split the country and destroy Confederation:

> I oppose this bill because it has in it the seeds of discord and disunion, because it is an obstacle and a bar to that union of heart and soul without which it is impossible to hope that this Confederation will attain the aims and ends that were had in view when Confederation was effected. Sir, all my life I have fought coercion; all my life I have promoted union.

Across the country the debate raged. Quebec's chief spokesperson, the fiery editor Henri Bourassa, wrote in his newspaper, *Le Devoir:*

> All Canadians who want logically and effectively to oppose conscription ought to have the courage to say and to repeat everywhere, "No conscription, no enlistments: Canada has done enough."

Bourassa's chief objection was as a French Canadian. A great majority of those who volunteered were English speaking. English was also the language of command. In the First World War, little recognition was given to the use of the French language in the Canadian army. English-speaking recruiting officers, some of them Protestant ministers, were sent into the Quebec countryside. For the rural Quebec citizens, this seemed positive proof of a plot "to seduce French youth from their religion by sending them off among the English to die in England's wars" (A.R.M. Lower).

Meanwhile, the Manitoba and Ontario governments were refusing to allow French-speaking children to be educated in their own language. Ontario's "Regulation 17" restricted French education to the primary grades. This legislation was upheld by the Judicial Committee of the Privy Council in 1916, just before the conscription debate. In the eyes of the French-Canadian nationalist, therefore, going to war for England and France seemed far less important than fighting with the government at home. Once again, Henri Bourassa made his stand clear:

> Those who have undertaken to bleed Canada white to uphold the forces of England and France in Europe tell us occasionally that our first line of defence is in Flanders (Belgium). I say that our first line of defence is at Ottawa.

The English-speaking viewpoint was summed up by newspaper editor J.W. Dafoe of the *Winnipeg Free Press:*

> French Canadians have refused to play their part in this war (being the only known race of white men to quit). They try to excuse themselves by alleging that they have domestic grievances which should first be righted. That excuse, if true, would be contemptible. In the face of an emergency like this, domestic questions have to stand.

The Military Service Act was finally passed in August of 1917. Wilfrid Laurier, who had opposed it, lost many of his English-speaking Liberal Party MPs. They crossed over to join a new coalition "Union" government headed by Prime Minister Borden.

The Union government then passed the Wartime Elections Act. This took the vote away from conscientious objectors and from Canadian citizens of alien origin, such as Germans and Japanese. The Act gave the vote to women serving in the armed forces and to soldiers' wives, mothers, and sisters. The Union coalition easily won the general election of December, 1917.

The Military Service Act allowed the government to enlist all single men from 18 to 60 years of age. Opposition to conscription did not die quickly. In October, 1917, Ontario conscripted 125 250 men; among them, 118 000 tried to be exempted for one reason or another. This was surprising for a province which had strongly supported conscription.

Opposition to conscription was particularly vehement in rural areas and in the West. On the farms, labour was in critically short supply by 1917. Many farmers could ill afford to lose the help of their sons. Anna Smokorowsky tells of one incident in Gilbert Plains, Manitoba. The townspeople and farmers were very patriotic, but they were nearly all opposed to conscription:

> There was a lot of dislike for conscription. The farmers didn't like it, and the townspeople didn't like it. They felt that it should be volunteer: those that wanted to go should go.
> I remember one incident out on the farm, not far from the homestead where we lived. There was a family that had two boys — a father, a sister, and the two boys. This boy was out bindering, like doing the harvest. He was out on the field bindering, and the RCMP came, and they took him right off that binder and left the binder and the horses in the bush there. When the father came, the binder was empty, and he didn't know what had happened till a week or a few weeks later. That was bad because the farmers, the older people, felt that they should have their sons to look after this harvest that they were growing. . . .
> I know there was a big fight that the farmers put up: they wanted these boys on the land; they needed them; it was wrong to pick up these boys because who was going to work the land to feed the army and to feed the war?

In the end, conscription added only about 83 000 new recruits, and not many of them ever saw the front lines. Many felt that the Canadian government was not realistic in enforcing

In the long run, a democracy is judged by the way a majority treats a minority.

Pierre Elliot Trudeau

Protesting against Conscription

As opposition to conscription intensified in 1917, public protests such as this anti-conscription parade in Montreal became common occurrences throughout Quebec.

conscription. By the middle of 1917, nearly 450 000 Canadians had already volunteered to serve overseas. This, from a total population of only eight million, was a truly remarkable effort. Labour shortages throughout the economy had already become critical. There was just no greater contribution that could reasonably be made or asked for.

Conscription in World War II

In the Second World War, conscription once again became an issue. Prime Minister Mackenzie King, mindful of the experience of 1917, had originally promised not to impose compulsory overseas service. However, in 1940, the government introduced conscription for home service, for North American defence.

As voluntary enlistments fell, there was pressure to bring back conscription for overseas service. In 1942, the government asked Canadians to vote to release it from its promise of no conscription. Again, deep French-English divisions showed up. English-speaking Canadians granted release by a large majority, while French Canadians bitterly opposed it.

As it turned out, there was no military need for conscription for another two years. However, in 1944, heavy losses in France and Italy forced Prime Minister King to make a decision. First, he appealed to the home defence soldiers to volunteer for overseas service. This appeal was not very effective. After a serious crisis within his Cabinet, King gave in. The government announced in November, 1944, that it would make 16 000 home defence troops available for overseas service. Very few of these troops made it to the front before the war ended in May of 1945. Since that time, conscription has not been a significant issue in this country, largely because Canada has enjoyed the protection of powerful allies.

Ethnic Relations

In wartime, emotions run high. Dislike of the enemy, and of anyone identified with the enemy, is strong. Fear is close to the surface, and suspicions are easily aroused. During wartime, hostilities were often carried from the international battlegrounds and applied to the Canadians whose families originally came from the enemy countries. In the First World War, there were exaggerated press reports which publicized rumours and created monstrous stereotypes of the enemy. Horror stories of atrocities supposedly committed by enemy soldiers were as common in Germany as they were in Canada.

Anti-German demonstrations occurred across Canada as well as throughout other Allied countries. In Ontario, the city of Berlin had its name changed to Kitchener, to honour the British Secretary of War, Lord Kitchener. In the West, thousands of German and Ukrainian Canadians lost their jobs and were placed in internment camps. This was also happening in the United States.

In 1917, German immigrants who had become Canadian citizens lost their right to vote. In 1918, the government prohibited the printing of "any publication in any enemy language." This closed down many German-language newspapers. Canada's Chief Press Censor, Major E.J. Chambers, admitted that the government had no reason to believe that the German-language newspapers had been disloyal in any way. In a letter to one German editor, he wrote:

The greatest difficulty confronting you . . . in connection with the continued existence of your paper as a German publication, was the increasing antagonism of those sections of the population which are not German, which do not understand the German language, which . . . view all Germans and everything German with suspicion.

Do you think it is ever right to treat a Canadian citizen differently because he, his parents, or his grandparents immigrated from a country which is currently at war with Canada?

Forced Labour

Public Archives Canada C-45103

These Canadians, because of their Japanese heritage, lost all their possessions and rights of citizenship during the Second World War. This group was among the many who were sent to work in the sugar beet fields of Manitoba and Ontario.

When war broke out, many Canadians and people from other Allied nations were caught in enemy countries. They suffered the same fate that people of alien origin suffered here, and often a far worse one. Quite a number of Allied civilians were maimed for life or never lived to tell of their experiences in the Japanese internment camps in World War II. When a country goes to war, residents related to the enemy unjustly suffer.

A Victim of Wartime Emotions

Mr Spade, who was German, lived at two or four Jersey Avenue in Toronto. At that time we lived at number fourteen. This happened after supper because I didn't see it happen. I overheard them talking about it. But a whole gang of men came around and got him and took him over, out on Clinton Street — that was only about a couple of hundred feet (sixty metres) away from his house — and they tarred and feathered him. Why I don't know, though he never was in trouble of any kind that I know of. He was a carter, he had a horse and wagon. He worked steady, and he never would drink or anything like that. — *Howard Ainsworth*

As quoted in Daphne Read, Ed., *The Great War and Canadian Society* (Toronto: New Hogtown Press, 1978)

Summary

In the two world wars of this century, Canada gave to the limit of her human and material resources. Of the huge number of Canadian men and women who served overseas in wartime, about 100 000 never returned. This immense contribution by a relatively small population had a great impact on Canadian society.

In 1900, Canada's economy was based mainly on agricultural and other primary resources. By 1950, this country had become a leading industrialized, urban nation. It had also shed its somewhat colonial status at the turn of the century and had become an independent force in world affairs.

However, war caused many stresses on the Canadian home front. The conscription issue twice almost tore the country apart and caused long-lasting strained relationships between French and English Canadians. Recruitment activities, rationing, income tax, wage and price controls, and the pressure to buy war bonds, all placed new pressures upon the civilian population.

The wars brought about many other changes as well. Wartime needs produced a great growth in industry and technological know-how. These advances were later applied to serve the home market in peacetime. As well, the status of Canadian women improved during this period. Without women undertaking almost every conceivable job in wartime — as skilled factory workers, nurses, business employees, or tractor drivers — the economy would have been severely crippled and the Canadian war effort would have been weaker. With this major contribution, women's demands for social justice and political equality could no longer be ignored. Canadian women won the right to vote as well as the ability to work in many areas of the Canadian economy previously closed to them.

CHAPTER FIVE

Why Do We Remember?

Each year, in November, there is a sombre occurrence in every city, town, and small village across Canada. In the morning, on the eleventh hour of the eleventh day of the eleventh month, a bugler plays the sad, lonely notes of the Last Post. This is followed by a one-minute silence among the crowds gathered to pay tribute to the 100 000 Canadians who died in the two world wars. This day, on which we commemorate the loss and sacrifice of these Canadians, is called "Remembrance Day."

In Europe, and in other places throughout the world, memorials and cemeteries show the final resting places of most of the Canadians who died in the wars. Simple headstones with a single maple leaf mark the graves. Every soldier's grave is marked in the same way; it has the soldier's rank, regiment, date of death, and sometimes a short inscription provided by relatives in Canada.

Many of the Canadian dead had no known burial place at all. The names of 11 000 of these are inscribed on the ramparts of the massive Vimy Ridge Memorial, which commemorates 60 000 Canadians who died in the First World War. The Vimy Memorial soars high above the now peaceful French countryside on 60 ha of land given forever to the Canadian people by the people of France.

Today the graves of Canadian soldiers are well maintained and regularly visited. One observer at a recent ceremony at Goresbeek in Holland recently wrote:

> Before each Canadian grave, a Dutch child knelt and placed a small bouquet of daffodils and miniature crossed flags — one Canadian and one Dutch. They then stood and bowed their heads in silent prayer before the graves of more than two thousand young men who had helped to free their country.

The beginning of the end of war lies in remembrance.

Herman Wouk

Canadian War Memorial at Vimy, France

At the base of the memorial for Canada's First World War victims, these words appear: "To the Valour of Their Countrymen in the Great War and in Memory of Their Sixty Thousand Dead, This Monument Is Raised by the People of Canada."

The National War Memorial in Ottawa

A Moving Memorial to Canadians Who Fell in Battle at Passchendaele, Belgium

French Farmers Bury a Canadian Soldier during the Second World War   *Public Archives Canada 37100*

War would end if the dead could return.

Stanley Baldwin (British Prime Minister)

Someone You Know?

Lynda Carlson
Grade 7, Wiarton Public School

Ready to serve, with admirable nerve
   they joined our country's forces.
Amid turmoil, to country, loyal,
   became objects; war resources.

Leaving chums and kin with gallant grin,
   knowing they mightn't return,
Became various groups, referred to as troops,
   with attitudes not needing concern.

Uniformed and at attention, there was small mention
   of secret worries and pride
With faultless bravery, like loyal slavery,
   their prestige could not be denied.

They took their stand in a foreign land,
   with unfamiliar things around.
Even with fighting, and lonesomeness biting,
   they bravely stood their ground.

Letters being fingered, while homey thoughts lingered
   of family, friends and freedom to roam.
Hopes of the war's end and wounds to mend,
   so they could go back home.

The breaking of dawn, like light upon
   the souls of dying men,
With faces turned down, towards the ground,
   such light won't greet them again.

Their bodies, shaken, soon to be taken
   to a place with proper graves.
Minds, not to know, themselves as heroes,
   whose sacrifices were bravest of braves.

These things keep in mind that we'll not find
   their fighting was in vain.
If we don't remember the eleventh of November,
   there may be a war again.

First prize in the 1975 Remembrance Day Eassay and Poetry Contest of the Royal Canadian Legion, Ontario Provincial Command

What thoughts then do we think during those silent moments we reserve each year for those killed? What should we remember on those days, especially those of us who were not even born before the last World War ended? Certainly our thoughts will be different from those of our parents or grandparents, or even great-grandparents, who may well have known the tragedy of war at first hand. Many of us, if we searched back in our "family tree," could find that tragedy there.

The Human Cost of War

In both world wars, the loss of human life was tremendous. Canada, Australia, and New Zealand lost heavily in proportion to their populations, although not so heavily as the principal nations in Europe and Asia. In the First World War, Canada's losses were twice as bad in proportion to the population as they were in the Second World War. In fact, although six million more died in the Second World War, the average number of battle deaths per million population was actually less because of the rise in the world's population since the First World War and the better health care received by those who were wounded. The accompanying charts show how great the losses were for all the nations involved.

	World War Battle Deaths (1914-1918) 51.5 Months of War			Second World War (1939-1945) 71.4 Months of War	

NATION	TOTAL NUMBER KILLED	NUMBER KILLED PER MILLION POPULATION	NATION	TOTAL NUMBER KILLED	NUMBER KILLED PER MILLION POPULATION
Rumania	335 000	47 183	*Germany*	3 500 000	44 416
France	1 350 000	32 927	Soviet Union	7 500 000	43 988
Germany	1 800 000	26 866	*Rumania*	300 000	15 000
Austria-Hungary	1 200 000	22 642	*Japan*	1 000 000	14 164
Great Britain	908 000	19 654	New Zealand	17 300	10 813
Italy	650 000	18 466	*Finland*	42 000	10 769
Turkey	325 000	17 568	● Poland	320 000	9 169
Belgium	87 500	11 513	Great Britain	270 000	5 684
Serbia	48 000	10 667	France	210 000	5 109
Russia	1 700 000	10 494	*Hungary*	40 000	4 348
Canada	60 661	7 641	Australia	29 400	4 324
Bulgaria	14 000	2 917	Canada	39 300	3 447
Greece	5 000	1 852	United States	408 000	3 141
United States	126 000	1 313	China	1 350 000	2 495
Portugal	7 000	1 129	*Italy*	17 300	1 777
Japan	300	6	Bulgaria	10 000	1 568
			● Greece	10 000	1 408
			● Belgium	9 600	1 143
			South Africa	8 700	870
			● Holland	6 200	713
			● Norway	2 000	690
			● Ethiopia	5 000	500
			● Yugoslavia	5 000	325
TOTAL	9 000 000	14 137 (Average)	TOTAL	15 000 000	10 912 (Average)

Germany and its allies are in italics.

Australia, New Zealand, and India are included in the figures for Great Britain.

Nations in each war are ranked in order of number killed for each million of population *at that time*.

Axis powers are in italics.

● These countries were in the war for less than six months.

What does Remembrance Day mean to you?

What do other Canadians remember about Canada's participation in war?

Can civilian deaths ever be prevented in modern warfare? Explain.

Civilian Deaths in Wartime

Before World War I, there were more provisions for protecting civilians during warfare. As late as 1910, all the great world powers signed an international agreement at The Hague, Holland, entitled *Laws and Customs of War on Land.* Here are some excerpts from it:

Article 17. In sieges and bombardments all necessary steps must be taken to spare, as far as possible, buildings dedicated to public worship, art, science, or charitable purposes, historic monuments, hospitals, and places where the sick and wounded are collected, provided they are not being used at the time for military purposes.

It is the duty of the besieged to indicate such buildings or places by distinctive and visible signs, which shall be notified to the enemy beforehand.

Article 25. The attack or bombardment, by any means whatever, of undefended towns, villages, dwellings, or buildings is forbidden.

Article 50. No collective penalty, pecuniary or otherwise, shall be inflicted upon the population on account of the acts of individuals for which it cannot be regarded as collectively responsible.

This international agreement was ignored four years later, during the First World War. And since that time, civilian deaths in wartime have skyrocketed. In the Second World War, more non-combatant men, women, and children were killed than soldiers. If we were to include deaths related to disease and famine caused by the wars, the civilian death rate would rise even higher. Some experts estimate that it would equal 30 million civilian deaths in the First World War and 45 million in the Second World War.

All this adds up to at least 100 million persons dead as a result of the wars; and it does not include the millions who were maimed and crippled for life. In the Soviet Union alone, the total population went down by 20 million during the Second World War. Losses were comparable in other nations.

Atomic Bombs

On August 6, 1945, the United States dropped an atomic bomb on the Japanese city of Hiroshima, instantly killing 76 000 people. On August 9, a second atomic bomb was dropped on Nagasaki, killing 80 000. Those who later died from wounds, radiation burns, or leukemia have never been counted.

The spectacular advances in science and technology in this century have greatly increased our destructive power. We have gone from the swords and lances of the Middle Ages to a single bomb which in seconds can kill 150 000 people. We no longer count our human losses in terms of how many military personnel have died. Now we count them also in terms of how many thousands of innocent civilians have lost their lives.

Even before the atomic bombs were dropped by the United States, there were massive bombings of such cities as Coventry, London, Dresden, Berlin, Tokyo, Rotterdam, and Warsaw. Four-fifths of all the bombs used in the entire Second World War were dropped on Germany when the end of the war was certain.

The way to win an atomic war is to make certain it never starts.

U.S. General Omar Bradley

World War II leaders condoned the killing of defenceless civilians. And the trend has continued. In the Vietnam war, civilian casualties far outnumbered military ones. The use of "anti-people" weapons such as napalm and the "wasting" of whole villages became common. Now in the event of nuclear war, it is estimated that 99 per cent of those killed would be civilians.

Why should we remember and talk about war? It is because only by understanding war will we each, individually, do our utmost to prevent it in the future. The world has more violence and war every day. In order to survive, we have to learn how to curb the violence in ourselves. Our Canadian experience in war is enough to strengthen our determination for peace. With atomic power now on the scene, the world

Military and Civilian Deaths in World War II

	ESTIMATED NUMBER OF DEAD
Russian soldiers killed in battle	5 500 000
Jews murdered in Nazi concentration camps	5 500 000
German soldiers killed in battle	3 500 000
Polish civilians murdered by the Nazis	3,000 000
Chinese military and civilian deaths	2 500 000
Russian prisoners-of-war murdered by the Nazis	2 500 000
Russian civilians murdered by the Nazis	2 000 000
European soldiers other than Germans or Russians killed in battle	2 000 000
Japanese soldiers killed in battle	1 500 000
Yugoslav civilians murdered by the Nazis	1 300 000
Russian civilians dead of starvation and bombardment in the siege of Leningrad	800 000
Austrian, Italian, Hungarian, Rumanian, Dutch, Belgian, Bulgarian, and Finnish civilian dead	600 000
Japanese civilians killed in American bombing raids	550 000
German civilians killed in Anglo-American bombing raids	550 000
British and British Empire soldiers killed in battle	500 000
American soldiers killed in battle	300 000
Czech civilians murdered by the Nazis	250 000
Greek civilians murdered by the Nazis	140 000
British civilians killed in German air raids	60 000
TOTAL WAR DEAD	**(Approximately) 33 000 000**

**The Mushroom Cloud of an Early Nuclear Explosion
at Bikini Island in the Pacific Ocean**

Old ships were placed at sea to measure the bomb's destructive power. Today's hydrogen bombs are far more destructive.

The Terrible Destruction of War

Either war is finished, or we are.

Victor Henry

must avoid any further conflict. As one modern philosopher writes:

> If I were asked to name the most important date in the history . . . of the human race, I would answer without hesitation, 6 August 1945. The reason is simple. From the dawn of consciousness until 6 August 1945, man had to live with the prospect of his death as an *individual;* since the day when the first atomic bomb outshone the sun over Hiroshima, mankind as a whole has had to live with the prospect of its extinction as a species. . . .
>
> In no earlier age did a tribe or nation possess the necessary equipment to make this planet unfit for life. They could inflict only limited damage on their adversaries. . . . Now they can hold the entire biosphere to ransom. A Hitler, born twenty years later, would probably have done so, provoking a nuclear Gotterdammerung. . . .
>
> Since the year zero . . . man has carried a time-bomb fastened round his neck, and will have to listen to its ticking — now louder, now softer, now louder again — until it either blows up, or he succeeds in defusing it. Time is running short, history is accelerating along dizzy exponential curves, and reason tells us that the chances of a successful defusing operation before it is too late are slender.

Arthur Koestler, Janus: A Summing Up (New York: Random House)

Public Archives Toronto

Scenes from the Shocking Atomic Destruction of the City of Hiroshima, August 6, 1945

Summary

What do we remember about the wars? Do we recall the 100 000 young Canadians who never came back or the many more who returned wounded, sometimes crippled for life? Do we ask what purpose or meaning was in their deaths, or do we just contemplate the tragedy of young men dead? What is the meaning of these deaths for us today? Do we realize our good fortune to live in a country as rich as Canada, a nation which has known no war on its own soil for over 150 years?

Do we remember the horror and destructiveness of wars in this century, not only for Canadians but for all the world's people? Why have we treated one another so violently — 75 million civilians and 25 million soldiers dead in two world wars? Do we also remember the countless millions who died simply because they were identified with a religious or cultural background unacceptable to their murderers?

Finally, do we resolve to take a stand individually and together as Canadians against human violence and further warfare, and to strive to prevent them whenever possible?

GLOSSARY

Anti-semitism   The support for views or practices directed against the interests, legal rights, religious beliefs, or the lives of Jewish people.

Aryan race   A cornerstone of Nazi policy was a belief in the racial superiority of a "master race," of which the best example was said to be the German people.

Genocide   The deliberate persecution and destruction of an entire ethnic group.

Ghetto   Specific sections of cities to which Jews and other persecuted groups are confined. This was common, especially in eastern Europe, prior to the Second World War.

Mobilization   The intensive preparation of a nation's armed forces for a possible war.

Monarchy   A state ruled by a king, queen, or emperor. A monarchy may be either democratic and constitutional or absolute (without checks on the ruler's power).

Fascism   An authoritarian, nationalistic, undemocratic, and anti-communist political movement which grew rapidly in Italy in the early 1920s. The term was also applied to similar movements in Germany and Spain.

Nazism   An abbreviation for the National Socialist German Workers Party, founded in 1919 as a reaction to the Versailles Treaty and taken over in the 1920s by Adolf Hitler. It espoused his unique fascist ideals — a mixture of extreme nationalism, anti-semitism, and social intolerance.

Refugees   People seeking safety in another country to escape religious, racial, or political persecution.

Republic   A state in which the people themselves control the government through constitutional representation.

Third Reich   The name given to the twelve-year dictatorship (1933-1945) of Adolf Hitler in Germany.

Totalitarian   A type of political system dominated by a single party which allows no opposition and severely restricts economic, social, and individual freedom.

Trench Warfare   A form of warfare in which opposing armies face each other on a long front in a complex series of trenches.

Versailles Treaty (1919)   Leaders of the victorious nations of the First World War met at Versailles, outside of Paris, to draw up a harsh peace treaty which they forced Germany to sign.